D1132130

END
OF THE
WORLD

A play by

ARTHUR KOPIT

A Mermaid Dramabook

🖑 HILL and WANG

A division of Farrar, Straus and Giroux

NEW YORK

for Audrey Wood

End of the World was first performed at the Kennedy Center in Washington, D.C., on March 28, 1984, and subsequently opened in New York at the Music Box Theater on May 6, with the following cast:

Michael Trent	John Shea
Philip Stone	Barnard Hughes
Audrey Wood	Linda Hunt
Paul Cowan	Richard Seff
Merv Rosenblatt	David O'Brien
Stella	Elaine Petricoff
General Wilmer	David O'Brien
Stanley Berent	Jaroslav Stremien
Pete	Peter Zapp
Jim	Nathaniel Ritch
Ann	Elaine Petricoff
Trent's Son	Wade Raley

Strangers, Charles, Waiters Waitresses, Attaché, Customers	Larry Pine, Elaine Petricoff, Nathaniel Ritch, Peter Zapp, Frank Hankey

Produced by the Kennedy Center and
Michael Frazier

Directed by Harold Prince
Scenery by Clarke Dunham
Costumes by William Ivey Long
Lighting by Ken Billington
Sound by Rob Gorton
Music by Larry Grossman

End of the World was inspired by an idea initiated by Leonard Davis.

AUTHOR'S NOTE

This play derives from real events. In the spring of 1981 I was approached by Leonard Davis, who wished to commission me to write a play about nuclear proliferation, based on a scenario he had written. Between that day and August 1983 I worked on the project—although not on his scenario—which turned out to be very different from his scenario. The events that unfold in my play mirror, almost exactly, the experiences I had when I embarked on the commission.

Much of the play—in particular the section entitled "The Investigation"—is based on personal interviews. Though some of those interviewed asked that they not be named, those who can be named include Walter Slocum, Fritz Ermath, Joel Resnick, Douglas Olin, Ambassador Edward Rowny, and Kurt Guthe. I would like to thank all of them for their patience, time and generosity.

Those whose written work proved especially valuable in the creation of this play and in my understanding of the issues involved include Herman Kahn, Freeman Dyson, Colin Gray, Keith Payne, Jack Geiger, Jonathan Schell, George Kennan, Richard Pipes, and Edward Teller.

In particular I wish to thank Roger Molander for his extraordinary help and encouragement during the writing of this play, and Robert Scheer for allowing me to use an extensive section of his book *With Enough Shovels,* published by Random House, as the basis for Philip Stone's final speech. I would also like to thank Physicians for Social Responsibility for their continued support.

A word about Audrey Wood. Audrey Wood was my agent

from 1960, when my play *Oh Dad, Poor Dad, Mamma's Hung You in the Closet and I'm Feelin' So Sad* was produced at Harvard, until 1981, when she suffered a devastating massive stroke. She was a crucial, integral, and loving part of my life. When I came to the writing of this play and found I needed to write in an agent for Michael Trent, my playwright/detective, I instinctively used Audrey's name, never intending to keep her name in the play. But I have done so.

I kept it in while writing it in the belief that her presence, as I went along, would force me to delve into the material and into myself as deeply as I could—for to do any less would be to belittle her.

And I kept it in in the hope that what I wrote might, in some small way, measure up to the measure of her.

A.K.

The Commission

MUSIC: *lazy, bluesy music for a hard-boiled detective. It is "Trent's Theme." Curtain up.*

SPOTLIGHT *up on* MICHAEL TRENT, *downstage, in a trench coat. Stage dark around him. He puffs on a cigarette. The music continues under.*

TRENT: I have now, at most, two hours left—two hours to solve a mystery which so far seems to yield no solution. If I fail, it is highly possible that I and all of you will die sooner than we'd hoped. Do I exaggerate? Of course. That is my method. I am a playwright. My name is Trent, Michael Trent. I work out of Stamford, Connecticut—that's where my office is, that's where this case began, when Philip Stone came to see me with a notion for a play. Generally I don't take commissions. This time I did.

Lights up on PHILIP STONE, *a man in his sixties, large, elegant, powerful.*

STONE: I can only tell you it is a matter of great urgency, and I would be most appreciative if I could see you tonight!

Blackout on STONE.

TRENT: I'd never met the man, though I knew of course who he was—who didn't? He told me what he wanted, which was a play, but gave no details. He assured me he'd pay well—a man as rich as Stone ought to pay well; I told him to come right out. To put it mildly, I was in great need of money at the time. Most playwrights need money *all* the time. It's not one of your top-paying professions. Besides, I had a wife, a kid, and two golden retrievers to support. As things now stand, you won't see any one of them. I want to keep them out of this!

Lights up on TRENT's *office in Stamford, Connecticut. It looks like the sort of office Philip Marlowe might use. On the glass door, reversed, are the following words:*

MICHAEL TRENT, PLAYWRIGHT
—No Domestic Comedies—

This is my office. At least, as it looked ten months ago, on the night Stone came by and changed my life irrevocably. Actually, in *real* life, where these events occurred, it doesn't look like this at all. Neither do the characters who were, and still are, involved. I have altered these details, not so much to protect the innocent, as to heighten interest. That's how playwrights work. We've got limited time. You don't want to stay here all night any more than I do. *(A buzzer sounds on* TRENT's *cluttered desk)* Yah!

STELLA *(Voice only):* Mike, there's a guy out here says his name is, get this—Philip Stone! *(Sound of* STELLA *giggling)*

TRENT: Hey, dollface, this guy *is* Philip Stone. Tell him I'll be with him in a minute. *(To audience)* It was important that Stone think I was in the middle of a project. If he didn't, he might figure he could get me cheap. My pulse was going wild; I'd been hoping to sell out for years. This could be it. *(Into the intercom)* Send Stone in. *(Back to audience)* Actually, I didn't even have a secretary. And that's all I'm going to tell you. From here on, you're going to have to figure out what I'm making up, and what I'm not, on your own. Be warned: the roads are very slippery, the ones we're going on tonight.

TRENT *starts typing. The office door opens and* PHILIP STONE *walks in. Black greatcoat. Sense of mystery and menace.*

STONE: Trent?

TRENT *(Typing wildly):* Just a second, be right with you, finishing touches here. Yes . . . Yes-yes, good, hah-hah, amazing, what a scene, never *seen* a scene like this!

STONE: Perhaps the moment is inopportune.

TRENT: NO! No-no, almost finished! Last few lines. Real bitch, this play; been working on it for a year—commission from the RSC. There! Yes! Got it! Beginning to think I'd *never* get it right! *(Rips the page from the typewriter, rises, and goes over to* STONE, *hand extended)* Mr. Stone, Michael Trent. Great honor to meet you. *(Into the intercom)* Stella, hold my calls. *(To* STONE) Can I offer you a drink?

STONE: Thank you. Yes. A Scotch would be welcome, most welcome indeed.

TRENT: All I've got is beer.

STONE: I'll stay like this . . . Mr. Trent, I am not a man who wastes words or time; words take time to say, time is precious. I have conceived an outline for a play. I wish to see this play produced, and quickly. I will provide the capital, you will write it. How much do you want, when can you begin?

Stunned pause. Then TRENT *rushes to the door.*

TRENT: Stella!

Enter STELLA, *a real dish.*

STELLA: Yes, boss!

TRENT: Be an angel. Run down to B.J.'s and get a bottle of Scotch.

STELLA: Right, boss!

Exit STELLA.

TRENT *(To audience):* If you're going to invent a secretary, might as well go with it all the way! *(To* STONE, *trying to control his euphoria)* Well, this is just very . . . very flattering. Let me check my appointment book here, see what sort of commissions I've got lined up. *(Rummages through the mess on his desk; he finds the appointment book)* Here it is. Let's see now . . . *(Flips the pages)* And you say you want this play written . . . ?

STONE: Right away!

TRENT: Right away, I see . . . Well, I could shuffle this, I guess. Delay this commission here . . . Might have to give up some work over here, that's something I really wanted too, *damn!* What, uh, kind of dollars exactly are we, uh, talking about?

STONE: As I said before, sir, tell me what you want.

TRENT: (So I *did* hear him right!) *What I WANT!* Well, that's not so . . . easy to say. It depends very much on how long this will take to *write.* Then to *re*write! . . . Then to rewrite *that* revision! I do very careful work, I'm sure you've heard. Then of course we have to factor in the research. If this project, I don't know it yet, takes research of some sort—

STONE: It will.

TRENT: There you are! So *that* must be factored in. Plus of course transportation, limousine, mind you now I don't absolutely *need* a limousine—

STONE: I use a limousine. No reason you should not.

TRENT: My God, the theater needs men like you!

STONE: Don't you want to hear the idea?

TRENT: No. No-no, I'll just begin. Obviously, if it matters all this much to you, it's got to be worth *something!* I'll need a day or two to figure out the terms, of course. Where can you be reached? You seem to have appeared a bit out of thin air.

STONE *(Handing him a card):* My business card.

TRENT: Good. Thank you. Well! I don't see that we need to discuss this any further—you've got yourself a playwright! I've got myself a producer! (STONE *holds out a manilla envelope)* This the idea?

STONE: Yes.

TRENT: Well, I can't wait to read it!

STONE: Why not read it now?

TRENT: Well, because right now I just can't give it my complete attention. We'll talk tomorrow. Sir, a great, *great* pleasure meeting you! (TRENT *ushers him out)* Till tomorrow.

STONE: Till tomorrow.

Exit STONE.

TRENT *(To audience):* I didn't want to look at his idea while he was here in case I hated it.

The door opens. STONE *pops back in.*

STONE: Sir. Forgive me. But in my excitement I forgot to give you this . . . *(Hands* TRENT *an envelope)* . . . *retainer.* As a token of good faith. *(Leaves)*

TRENT *tears open the envelope. He pulls out five bills.*

TRENT: *Five thousand dollars!* (Opens the door) SIR, YOU ARE TOO GENEROUS!

STONE *(Offstage):* What?

TRENT: *That* was the wrong thing to say. I meant to say, MAYBE WE CAN DO SOME *MORE* PLAYS! YOU KNOW —AFTER THIS! *(To the audience)* Five thousand dollars! . . . Well, it may not seem like a lot to you. But to a playwright, as an advance, it's enough to save his life. It really is.

Enter STONE, *somber-faced.*

STONE: Sir, you do not understand. I have no interest in producing plays. I am interested in producing one play only. *This is it!*

Exit STONE.

TRENT *clearly taken aback by this. Nervously, he opens the manila envelope and peeks inside. Cautiously, he slides the pages out. He stares down at the title page. Then he stares out with a look of alarm.*

Blackout.

Lights up on AUDREY WOOD, TRENT's *agent. She is a woman in her sixties. Very short. She wears a tiny pillbox hat. She is hardly visible above her desk. At the moment, she is talking on the phone with* TRENT.

AUDREY: Dear, I checked him out. He's legitimate, he has the money. So I'd say you've got a deal.

TRENT: Audrey, his idea is terrible!

AUDREY: Then don't take it.

TRENT: How can I not take a deal like this? This is a definitional sweetheart deal, this is the deal of a lifetime!

AUDREY: Dear, what do you want me to do?

TRENT: ADVISE me!

AUDREY: Take the deal.

TRENT: Audrey, you don't understand. You haven't read this man's scenario. There is no way anyone, ANYONE! can write a play based on this. Do you know why? Because the characters are completely cardboard, and the plot preposterous.

AUDREY: Dear, listen, calm down, brush your hair, make yourself presentable, come in and show me this notorious scenario. I'm sure it's not half as bad as you think. Really, dear, you're still young, you've got a lovely wife, a lovely child, this is no time to panic.

TRENT: I've used up the advance.

Pause.

AUDREY: *What?*

TRENT: *I've used up the advance.*

AUDREY: Darling, I'm sorry, I must have misunderstood. I thought you got this advance last night.

TRENT: I did.

She checks her watch.

AUDREY: Dear, it is ten-thirty in the morning. What do you *do* up there in Connecticut?

TRENT: Audrey, I used it to pay our mortgage. We owed three months—I'm sorry, that's the way it is—we're going through a rough time here.

AUDREY: Maybe you should go out to the Coast.

TRENT: I DON'T WANT TO *GO* TO THE COAST! I'LL START TAKING MORE DRUGS THAN I'M TAKING NOW!

AUDREY: Darling, you mustn't take drugs. It's bad for your health.

TRENT: I'll see you this afternoon.

AUDREY: Dear, I'm afraid you may have to take this deal.

TRENT: I'll see you this after— *(But* AUDREY *has already clicked off)* —noon. *(Lights off on* AUDREY. TRENT *turns to the audience)* Okay, I know exactly what you're thinking: Where is the problem? You take the money, you write what you can, the play's no good, no one does the play, you've got your money, basta! end of deal. If I could actually count on that, you're right, no problem. Here's the hitch: this guy is so rich he's liable to produce this play no matter *how* bad it is! Why should this matter?

AUDREY'S ASSISTANT *(Voice only):* Miss Wood will see you now.

TRENT: One second! I'll be right with her. *(To audience)* People who write plays are a little crazy, okay? For one thing, no one writes plays to make money. I mean you *do,* of course. But you don't go into it, as a profession, because that's where you figure the big bucks lie. You do it . . . and you spend your life doing it, because it *matters.* And you have a kind of pact with yourself. And it says you don't screw around with what matters or else it's gone.

AUDREY'S ASSISTANT *(Voice only):* Miss Wood will see you now!

TRENT: Yes, yes. Coming!

Lights back up on AUDREY. TRENT *walks over, manila envelope in hand.*

AUDREY: Dear, if you want to get out of this, I'll loan you the money.

TRENT: No, I can't do that.

AUDREY: Of course you can, don't be a fool.

TRENT: Look, here's his scenario. Four pages. Actually, only three. The first page is taken by the title.

AUDREY: What's the title?

TRENT: *The End of the World.*

AUDREY: Ohhhh, dear.

TRENT: You know what it deals with?

AUDREY: I was afraid to ask.

TRENT: Nuclear proliferation.

AUDREY: Oh dear, oh dear, oh dear.

TRENT: I mean, is that an exciting subject or isn't it?

AUDREY: Why does he want to *do* this play?

TRENT: No idea.

AUDREY: Well, let's call him up! *(Buzzing her intercom)* Get me Philip Stone. Bob Montgomery has his number. *(Back to* TRENT*)* Montgomery's his lawyer. He called after you did. Stone will agree to whatever terms you want.

TRENT: The man is mad!

AUDREY: That's no reason not to work with him. *(The intercom buzzes)* Yes?

AUDREY'S ASSISTANT *(Voice only):* Philip Stone on the line.

AUDREY *(Into phone):* Philip Stone? Audrey Wood—I am Michael Trent's agent. I gather you met with my client last night. Mr. Trent is sitting here with me in my office now. *(To* TRENT*)* Say hello, dear.

TRENT *(Picking up a second phone):* Hello!

Lights up on STONE, *on the phone.*

STONE: Hello!

AUDREY *(Into phone):* Dear, we would like to know why you're so anxious to produce this particular play.

STONE: I want to produce it because I believe the earth is doomed.

AUDREY: I'm sorry . . . *What?*

STONE: Doomed! I believe the earth is doomed!

AUDREY *stares at* TRENT.

AUDREY: He *is* mad! *(Into phone)* Mr. Stone, I'm sorry, are you suggesting that a production of your play could prevent this doom?

STONE: Yes, I think perhaps it could.

TRENT *(Sotto voce):* Ask him if he's planning on road companies.

She waves him off.

AUDREY: Well, dear, I must say this is certainly one of the *worthiest* projects I've come across in a very long time.

STONE: Possibly ever.

AUDREY: . . . Yes. Possibly ever. *(To* TRENT, *sotto voce) You've got to get out of this! (Back to* STONE) Darling, you still there?

STONE: Still here!

AUDREY: How long would you say we have till doom strikes?

STONE: My statistics suggest it could be almost any time.

AUDREY: So then you'll be anxious to get it on this season.

STONE: I was hoping for this spring.

AUDREY *(To* TRENT): I've never heard of anything like this. *(Back into phone)* I take it you've never produced before.

STONE: No.

AUDREY: Well, you have to be prepared for this play closing. Rapidly.

STONE: Why?

AUDREY: Well, I think there's a good chance audiences may not like it. Just by definition. Frankly, unless I'm missing some essential elements, it sounds rather *downbeat* to me.

STONE: I'm sorry, I don't understand. If audiences don't like it, do I *have* to close the play?

AUDREY *(Stunned):* Well . . . no, of course not.

STONE: Then I won't.

AUDREY: But what if no one comes?

STONE: No one at *all?*

AUDREY: Dear, it's been known to happen!

STONE: I find it hard to believe someone would not come in *eventually.* (AUDREY *and* TRENT *stare at each other in astonishment)* In the winter, for example. It's *warm* inside a theater. People are bound to come in . . . No, I'm going to keep this thing running. The earth's future is at stake! One doesn't close a play when the earth's future is at stake.

AUDREY *(To* TRENT, *sotto voce): We've got to keep this man to ourselves! (Back to* STONE) Dear, I think this is one of the most unusual and worthwhile projects I've ever come across. Hold on a sec. *(Cups her hand over the mouthpiece)* What if he really *knows* something here?

TRENT: What do you mean?

AUDREY: About the earth! About its doom!

TRENT: Oh, my God.

AUDREY: Dear, listen, why take a chance? *Talk* with the man. If a play of yours could in some way help prevent global doom, well!

TRENT: Oh, my God!

AUDREY *(Into the phone):* If you like, my client will meet with you this afternoon.

Blackout on AUDREY *and* STONE.

TRENT *(To audience):* I was, of course, an innocent . . . As I soon found out.

Lights up on STONE.

STONE: To put it mildly, sir, I am thrilled by your stopping by. Already I feel hope rising in my breast. Charles! Some drinks! Scotch, if you like; we have it.

TRENT *(To audience):* I told him I wanted nothing.

STONE: Good. All business. For me, then, nothing either.

TRENT *(To audience):* Stone had requested that the meeting be at his place. Now I was in his apartment. (STONE*'s sumptuous Fifth Avenue apartment glides into view*) If I'd ever wanted booze this was it, but something warned me. I sensed a need for clearheadedness: the height had already made me dizzy enough. As a rule, I dislike elevators. For some reason, I cannot rid my mind of the image of what lies underneath as I ascend. Because of this, whenever possible, I walk upstairs. Stone lived in a penthouse forty floors up. There is a limit to any neurosis; forty floors was mine. Now the world was reeling. Looking down through the half-opened window of Stone's library, which I desperately did not *want* to do but felt myself *compelled* to do, I saw the people on the streets below wobbling like rubber. Like dolls made of rubber. The buildings were also like rubber. And, in the hot summer sun, seemed to be *melting!*

STONE *(Coming up behind him):* Extraordinary perspective from up here.

TRENT: . . . Yes.

STONE: Why don't you sit down?

TRENT: Thank you. (STONE *leads him to a seat. To audience)* And I missed the seat!

TRENT, *in sitting, indeed misses the seat. He lands on the floor like a clown. Stunned expression. Beat.*

Blackout.

Lights up on AUDREY.

AUDREY *(To audience): What does an agent do? (Pause)* This is a question I am asked all the time . . . In *theory,* an agent is supposed to find her client *work* . . . Now, while this has certainly been *known* to happen, fortunately, for all concerned, we do much, much more. Take this instance here. Michael Trent had been my client now for nearly fifteen years, and, relatively speaking, we'd done well together; though he wasn't rich, neither was he starving. Comfortable, I would say, is what he was—till recently . . . Now, all writers go through down periods; this was something more. What worried me about Michael was his growing eccentricity. He imagined himself as a kind of *detective!* Even on the hottest, brightest summer day he would wear a trench coat, collar up; slouch hat, brim down! Frankly, he looked ridiculous. Well, I'm very fond of him. And consider it my job to protect him from harm . . . Anyway, when this Stone project came along, though financially the deal was incredible, unprecedented, something just said to me, *Audrey, watch out!* I decided I needed help . . . So I called a meeting: Merv Rosenblatt—he's the president of our agency, and Paul Cowan, Agent to the Stars! Paul refused to come downstairs to *my* office, I refused to go up to *his,* so we agreed to meet for lunch at the Russian Tea Room. *(A booth from the Russian Tea Room glides on)* Paul was the first to arrive—*(Enter* PAUL COWAN, *in sweat suit)*—dressed in his normal dapper style.

PAUL *(Sullenly):* Hi, Audrey. *(Slides in next to her and starts chewing on a napkin)*

AUDREY: Merv Rosenblatt came next. *(Enter* MERV ROSEN-BLATT, *in sharp, pinstriped suit with carnation in lapel. He is suntanned)* He'd canceled a lunch with Frank Purdue, that's how important this meeting was!

MERV: Okay, what's this about global doom?

PAUL: I'm sure it's an exaggeration.

MERV: Hi, Paul. Hope that's not a contract you're chewing on.

PAUL: No-no. Napkin. Listen, why don't we get started. I've got a screening in twenty minutes. *(To someone unseen by us)* Hey! I'll be in till seven, gimme a call! *(To someone else)* Hi! *(Back to* AUDREY) Sorry, Audrey. Go ahead.

AUDREY: Gentlemen. At this very instant, not ten blocks from here, my client is meeting with Philip Stone.

PAUL: Who's he?

AUDREY: Paul, I sent you a memo on *all* of this!

PAUL: Well, I can't remember! What are we, playing games?

AUDREY: Philip Stone is the man who's vowed to keep my client's play running no matter what.

PAUL: Right. Now I remember! This is the kind of producer our theater NEEDS! Mervin, what would you like?

MERV: Campari and soda.

PAUL: CAMPARI AND SODA AND A BLOODY MARY! Now, when can I meet this guy?

AUDREY: Well—

HEADWAITER: PHONE CALL FOR MR. COWAN!

PAUL: Bring it here!

MERV: Isn't Stone the guy who says we're doomed?

AUDREY: He's the one.

MERV: Well, that's *not* the kind of producer our theater needs! What the hell's Paul talking about?

HEADWAITER *(Arriving with plug-in phone):* Here you are, Mr. Cowan.

PAUL: You think I'm gonna plug it in? Plug it in.

The WAITER *climbs over* MERV.

MERV *(From beneath the* WAITER*):* Paul, is this really necessary?

PAUL: How do I know? *(The* WAITER *climbs back out.* PAUL *picks up the phone. To the others)* Keep talking; I can listen. *(Starts scribbling on the tablecloth)*

AUDREY: Stone says he's willing to pay anything my client wants.

PAUL *(Still on phone):* Maybe it's a project Paramount would like.

AUDREY: I've read Stone's scenario and it's terrible.

PAUL: Why don't we let Paramount decide.

AUDREY: It's about nuclear war.

PAUL *(Into phone):* Hold on. *(To* AUDREY*)* Paramount will only consider projects about nuclear war if there's an upbeat ending.

AUDREY: This has no ending whatsoever.

PAUL: Well, that, I would say, is a problem. *(Back into phone)* Yeah. Go ahead. *(Continues scribbling on the tablecloth)*

AUDREY: My instinct is to turn the project down.

PAUL: Are you mad?

AUDREY: Paul, I will not stand for rudeness! I am seeking advice, all right? *Seeking.* And I've brought you in on this as a courtesy.

PAUL: Mervin, talk to her.

MERV: Audrey, if your client turns this project down, how will we find out if the earth is doomed?

PAUL: Right! At least have him stay with this till we find out *that.* I've got deals pending here.

AUDREY: My client feels it is unethical to—

MERV: *What?*

AUDREY: *Unethical—*

PAUL *(Into phone):* Hold on. *(To* AUDREY*)* WHAT?

AUDREY: My client feels it is unethical to accept a deal knowing from the outset that there's no way it can be done.

PAUL *(Into phone):* Did you hear that? Can you believe what you're hearing here? *(To* AUDREY*)* So you're advising him to turn this *down?*

AUDREY: I'm not advising him to do *anything.*

PAUL: WELL, WHAT KIND OF GODDAMN ADVICE IS *THAT?*

MERV: Paul!

PAUL: Where the hell are our drinks? WOULD YOU PLEASE BRING OUR GODDAMN DRINKS! *(Into phone)* I better call you back. *(Hangs up. To* AUDREY*)* Audrey, look, far be it for me to butt into your affairs, but how much did your client earn last year?

AUDREY: Not a lot.

PAUL: I will personally guarantee him twice what he made just to keep this project alive. Mervin, are you in on this?

MERV: Well—

PAUL: Mervin's in. Audrey, all your client has to do is string this guy along. Meanwhile, we interest him in *other* worthy projects—I've got I'd say ten—and, simultaneously, find out if the earth is doomed. It if is, we make plans.

AUDREY: What sort of plans?

PAUL: How do I know? You just gave me this today!

MERV: When he says doomed, does he mean the West Coast, too?

AUDREY: I believe that's included, yes.

PAUL: You know I have to tell you, from the little I am gleaning here, this doesn't sound like what I'd call a box-office smash.

MERV: Well now, *Earthquake* did quite well.

PAUL: As a FILM? Hey, this could be sensational. But I understand he's talking drama, right?

AUDREY: Drama.

PAUL *(To* MERV*)*: We could take the Winter Garden after *Cats* is gone, blow the whole place up. I mean, it's halfway there already, right? *(To* AUDREY*)* What about this as a musical?

MERV: Paul!

PAUL: Don't reject things out of hand. *(To* AUDREY*)* Who are the main characters?

AUDREY: Well, the main one I would say is the President.

PAUL *(To* MERV*)*: Who could we get?

MERV *ponders.* PAUL *ponders. The same inspired casting idea hits them simultaneously.*

AUDREY: Gentlemen, Ron is President, right now!

PAUL: Well, when he LEAVES!

AUDREY: The man wants to do the play this spring.

MERV: Name the other characters, we can always cast the President.

AUDREY: There's only one other major character: the Soviet premier.

MERV *ponders.* PAUL *ponders.*

PAUL: Ann-Margret's looking for something.

AUDREY: Paul, the premier is a *man!*

PAUL: It's written that it cannot be a woman? Where? In what Russian document? I don't speak Russian; do you speak Russian? The British have a woman; why can't the Russians?

MERV: Audrey, Ann-Margret's a good idea.

PAUL: No, great idea, *great* idea! Look, the important thing is this: cast it right, I don't care what the thing's about, it runs! You want my advice? Your client *doesn't* take this deal. He *grabs* this deal! GRABS this deal!

MERV: And, meanwhile, finds out if the earth is doomed.

PAUL: Right. CHECK!

Blackout.

Lights up on TRENT, *still on the floor.* CHARLES *helps him to a chair.*

TRENT *(To* STONE): I don't know why . . . I suddenly felt quite dizzy.

STONE *(Warm and helpful):* Perhaps it was the open window
. . . Many people—perfectly *normal* people, people of a
sunny disposition—confronted suddenly by an open window,
all at once find themselves wondering if they shouldn't jump.
The notion takes their breath away. And they faint. Charles,
bring our guest some water. *(Exit* CHARLES*)* Now obviously
I'm not saying this was you.

TRENT: It certainly sounds that way.

STONE: Well, I'm only speculating. Anyway, I don't think you
were literally about to jump. I think you were just *thinking*
about jumping!

TRENT: I'm the most self-protective person you have ever
met!

STONE: That's why you fainted. Trent, look, why shilly-
shally? You're a man of imagination. How can you *look* at a
window and NOT think about jumping?

TRENT: I didn't realize that's what imagination led to.

STONE: For God's sake, man, the window was *open!* What do
you want, a written invitation?

TRENT: I think I'd like something stronger than water.

STONE: CHARLES!

CHARLES *(Reentering instantly):* You shouted?

STONE: Our guest would like something stronger than water.

CHARLES: I'm not surprised.

Exit CHARLES.

STONE: Now listen, Trent. If you're not going to be honest with me, *or* yourself, what's the point of our going on? In front of you is an open window; beyond, forty exhilarating floors below, *oblivion!* Now. How can you, as a normal human being, not at least *contemplate* jumping out?

TRENT: I don't contemplate jumping out because I'm not in *despair!*

STONE: What's despair got to do with this?

TRENT: I'd have thought everything.

STONE: I'm beginning to think you're some kind of ninny. Trent, listen to me. We are on the verge of beating a dead horse. I did *not* expect you to jump out the window, all right? In fact, to be perfectly fair, I'd have been astounded had you even stood on the LEDGE! The point is this. *(Enter CHARLES, rolling a cart filled with booze)* Ah, thank you, Charles. The point is this. (TRENT *hurries toward the cart)* Trent, are you listening?

TRENT *(Grabbing a bottle):* Avidly.

STONE: THE POINT IS THIS! (TRENT *starts to open it)* The urge to leap out of windows does not derive from despair. It derives from *curiosity.*

TRENT: . . . Curiosity?

STONE: Yes sir, curiosity, rampant curiosity! I myself feel the urge *all the time.* Fortunately, I resist . . . Fortunate for me. Fortunate for those down below. *(Grins)* Enough! On to business. Your agent informs me you have certain reservations about my scenario. If you'd be so kind, I'd like to hear what these reservations are; please speak freely, our relationship will founder if it isn't based on absolute, unwavering trust.

TRENT: Right. Uhhh, thank you. Well! I would say, offhand, that the single biggest problem with your scenario is that it's basically *implausible.*

STONE: It's *supposed* to be implausible.

TRENT: I see . . . Well, I didn't catch that.

STONE: Do you honestly think the next world war is going to start in some *plausible* way?

TRENT: No, I see what you mean.

STONE: In fact, *I* think this basic implausibility is the most plausible thing *in* my scenario . . . And I worked very hard to achieve it.

TRENT: Yes, well, you've succeeded.

STONE: So when can I expect a script? (TRENT *looks about as if for a way to escape)* You understand, I don't mean to rush you now, but time is clearly of the essence here, I'm sure you can see why.

TRENT: Doom, you mean.

STONE: Yes, sir, doom. Could be any moment now.

TRENT: Look, Stone, I've got to tell you something. The truth is, I just don't see doom in your scenario. I mean, I see *theatrical* doom. That's written all over the place. But historic doom? global doom? Can't seem to catch sight of it.

STONE: That's because it's not in.

TRENT: Not *in?*

STONE: My scenario.

TRENT: The global doom you are so concerned about is not IN your scenario?

STONE: That's correct.

TRENT: Well, don't you want to *put* it in?

STONE: No, sir!

TRENT: Why?

STONE: Because if I put in everything I know, no one will BELIEVE me, sir!

TRENT: But NO ONE WILL BELIEVE WHAT YOU'VE *GOT!*

STONE: By gad, we're at an impasse here!

TRENT: Maybe what we need is a new approach.

STONE: Good idea! What do you suggest?

TRENT: That you tell me what you know. And let *me* figure out how to dramatize it—how's that sound?

STONE: No, sir, I cannot.

TRENT: I thought our relationship was based on TRUST!

STONE: And so it is. And you're just going to have to trust me when I tell you doom approaches.

TRENT: Stone, listen. Let me explain something about basic dramatic construction: I cannot go out on the stage during my play and say to my audience, "Hey! Trust me! Doom approaches!" I have got to *convince* them that doom approaches. And how'm I going to do that if you can't convince ME?

STONE: It's a stickler.

TRENT: It's a stickler, absolutely right. Now, what I'm going to do—*(Downs his drink)*—is go home. *(Puts down his glass)* And let you think this whole thing over. It's been a fascinating afternoon. No need to show me to the door.

STONE: Trent! For God's sake, don't you understand? If I could just TELL you how I *know* doom is approaching, why, what's to stop me from telling *everyone?* You see? And then why would I need a play? I wouldn't!

TRENT: Stone. As I see it, there are only two possibilities here. Either you are certifiable. Or you're certifiable. In the first instance, you are certifiable because you've made all this up; in the second, you are certifiable because you *haven't* made it up but won't TALK! To this, I have but two possible responses. Out the door. And out the door. Farewell. Farewell.

STONE: No! Please, sir, you mustn't! Look, sir, I am on my knees! Future generations are on their knees!

TRENT: All I see is you.

STONE: That's because you are shortsighted, sir. You see only the immediate!

TRENT: No. I see a door, that's what I see. And I'm going through it!

STONE: Trent! *(Grabs* TRENT's *legs)* The fate of the world lies in your hands.

TRENT: Really? You know what? Fuck it! Let it blow!

STONE: It's attitudes like this, sir, that will do us in, attitudes like this!

TRENT: Hey! Hold on . . . I've just figured out the problem. You know the problem? I'm the wrong writer for this project! With the right writer, this project could just go ZOOM! What you must do, right away, is call my agent: she will send you another writer!

STONE: But you, sir, are the writer that I want.

TRENT: Wonderful! Why?

STONE: I can't tell you that.

TRENT: Stone, listen to me: if you don't let me out this door this instant, I am going to create, before your eyes, in this room, a doom such as you have never dreamed! (STONE *takes out a gun)* Oh, my God.

STONE: Now I suggest you sit down over there.

TRENT: HELP!

STONE: I am the only tenant on this floor.

TRENT: CHARLES!

STONE: Charles works for me; he's used to my behavior. Sir, please sit down. This is no frivolous enterprise! My life is in jeopardy. And, like it or not, so is yours. (TRENT *decides to sit)* Now. When I am done, if you still wish to leave my employ, you may do so. Furthermore, you may keep the money I have paid so far. How does that strike you, sir? Is that fairness or not?

TRENT: That . . . seems quite fair. Yes.

STONE: Good. So, with your permission, then, I will put this morbid instrument away.

TRENT: Oh. Yes. Please.

STONE: I find guns tend to have a will of their own! Fascinating creatures. I call this particular gun Fred.

TRENT: Fred! That's a *nice* name for a gun.

STONE: Yes, it is. It's strong. Guns *need* good strong names. You can get into all *kinds* of trouble if your gun doesn't have a good strong name. Donald, for example. That's a dreadful name for a gun!

TRENT: Yes. Yes, I can see that. Gun wouldn't *respect* you if you called it Donald.

STONE: Exactly! Gun like that could turn on you and *kill* you! Any moment! Have *you* ever had a gun?

TRENT: No. *(Pause)* Well. Actually, I once had a BB gun.

STONE: And what did you call it?

TRENT: Uhhhhhhh, Jim.

STONE: Jim! Yes, that's a *good* name for a gun.

TRENT *(Heading for the phone):* You know, I wonder, would you mind very much if I asked my agent to come over here?

STONE: No need, sir! We'll be through in a trice!

TRENT: Good.

STONE: Next time, though. Now, on to doom.

TRENT: Global doom!

STONE: Clear this whole thing up!

TRENT: Good.

STONE: Tell me, sir, what these ten countries have in common: India, Egypt, Iraq, Argentina, Israel, Japan, Korea, South Africa, Libya, Brazil.

TRENT: No idea.

STONE: Within ten years, sir, each of these countries will possess the bomb.

TRENT: Really!

STONE: Yes, sir.

TRENT: And to you this means we're doomed.

STONE: No, sir! No, not in and of itself. This is but the *clay* from which our doom will be shaped! Sculpted! Formed!

TRENT: You see doom as a work of *art?*

STONE: Yes sir. Exactly! And, to me, this is part of its *horror* . . . and *allure.* (STONE *smiles at* TRENT. TRENT *leans back and studies* STONE *with a new intensity. Sotto voce)* Now, the reason I believe doom approaches rapidly has to do with certain . . . *information* I stumbled upon quite by accident about a year ago, I shan't tell you how, not now at least . . . This information is at first blush so incredible that were I to simply tell you what it is, you would be bound not to believe it, just as I at first did not and in some ways still do not, *cannot!* though I know full well all of it is true. You see my dilemma here. If I tell you what I know, you will say Stone is mad, and leave. End of project, end of hope. On the other hand, if somehow you believe what I reveal, then I can only conclude that you are the one who's mad. So what am I to do? The answer's obvious. What I have come to know, on my own, you must somehow come to know on your own, as well . . . How?

. . . By proceeding systematically . . . and *following your nose.*

TRENT: My nose tells me to get out of here.

STONE: Of course! To save yourself from a terror such as you have never known! Why do your eyes dart toward the window, sir? That's no way out.

TRENT: *Why a play?*

STONE: Why, indeed! . . . Because the theater, sir, alone among the arts, engages, in equal measure, the emotion and the intellect. And both must be touched here, if we are to survive.

Silence.

TRENT: Why me?

STONE: As I said, sir: I cannot tell you that.

TRENT: *Why?*

STONE: Because at this moment, sir, your greatest strength is your innocence.

Pause.

TRENT: Well, I can't work like that, I'm sorry. (STONE *turns away*) All right. Look. I *will* work on this, okay? . . . BUT *only* if you tell me what it is about *my* plays that makes you think I am right for this job.

STONE: Well, sir, the truth is, and I hope you take this in the proper spirit—I've never actually *seen* a play of yours.

TRENT: WHAT?

STONE: But I've been assured they're very good.

TRENT: Stone, you are out of your goddamn mind!

STONE: No sir. Would that I were.

TRENT: Well, something's cuckoo here. And I think I'll leave before it's me! *(Starts out)*

STONE *(Drawing his gun):* Sorry, sir, I object. (TRENT *sees the gun and stops)* Sir, I am a desperate man! . . . But I am also a *gambling* man. I will gamble. I will tell you this: . . . *we have met before.*

TRENT *(Amazed): Where?*

STONE: I cannot tell you that.

TRENT: STONE, I CANNOT TAKE THESE GAMES ANYMORE! NOW, IF YOU WANT TO SHOOT ME, SHOOT ME, BUT THAT'S IT, GOODBYE!

STONE: SIR!

TRENT: *I don't recall meeting you, all right?*

STONE: I am aware.

TRENT: So how important could this meeting have been?

STONE: To me, crucial.

TRENT: When did this meeting take place?

STONE: I can't tell you that.

TRENT: How many were there?

STONE: I can't tell you that, either!

TRENT: I see! And yet, at this meeting, something happened which has convinced you I could save the world from doom!

STONE: Yes, sir. Absolutely!

TRENT: Aren't you a bit surprised I don't remember?

STONE: No, sir. I *thought* you might blot it out.

TRENT: BLOT IT *OUT?*

STONE: Yes, sir.

TRENT: If the incident was anything like this, of COURSE I've blotted it out! People must be blotting you from their lives all the time! I AM LEAVING!

STONE: All right, sir! All right! (TRENT *stops and turns back)* I will tell you this . . . but *only* this . . . More than this and my cause is lost. *(Pause)* This . . . particular incident . . . *convinced* me . . . that you, sir, had a thorough understanding of *evil.*

TRENT: . . . *I?*

STONE: Yes, sir. You. (TRENT *stares at him in astonishment)* And now, sir, it is *my* turn to leave. I hope you take this job. *(Warm smile)* Good day.

TRENT *turns to the audience. As he does, the light in the room fades almost to black. However, the sky beyond the open window does not dim at all. In this darkened room,* STONE, *unmoving, is a shadowy presence.*

TRENT: I had, of course, no idea what he meant. *(Pause)* I would say I took the job . . . because of *two* factors . . .

(Music: "Trent's Theme") One, of course, was the money. How could I turn down a deal like that? *(Takes out a cigarette)* And the other, of course, was curiosity.

Lights the cigarette. Puffs.

The light through the window has been growing brighter. Now, blazing white, it seems to beckon.

Curtain

The Investigation

MUSIC: *"Trent's Theme." It continues as lights come up on a seedy hotel room. It is night. Through the one window in this room, a red neon hotel sign is visible across the street; the sign says "Sunset Motel." Except for this light, the only other light in the room comes from a lamp.* TRENT, *in his trench coat, looks out at the audience*

TRENT: To be precise, ten months, five days, twelve hours, and . . . *(Checks his watch)* . . . twenty-three minutes have passed now since Philip Stone came into my life wielding a four-page scenario of dubious merit. Frankly, I've still no idea what he meant when he said I understood evil. As far as I know, I'm a pussycat, a sweetheart, aces—what the hell was he talking about? *(Puffs on a cigarette)* Not that I haven't uncovered some rather peculiar goings-on, you understand! No-no, quite the contrary, this case has been a real eye-opener! There's funny business going on out there, and I had no idea of it. Can't remember when I've been so depressed by a case. *(Pours a shot of bourbon)* And I've never made so much money, either. Tells you something about money, doesn't it. You know what it tells you? Tells you, without all this money I'd be even *more* depressed. By the way, this is Washington. The Pentagon's back that way. I was there early this morning. *(There is a soft rap on the door. He tenses)* I know it isn't Stella; Stella has a key. *(Sets his glass down quietly)* She came down on the six o'clock shuttle. About an hour ago, I sent her across the street to case the lobby of a two-bit fleabag called the Sunset Motel—*(Starts moving cautiously toward the window)*— where I'm supposed to meet with a man who claims he can clear up everything. A man who calls himself The Shadow— really, I'm not kidding, that's what the message said. Is Stone behind all this? If so, I've been set up. Why? *(Another rap.* TRENT *peers out through the half-opened slats of the Venetian blinds)* I can see the lobby from here. No sign of Stella.

MUFFLED VOICE *(Softly, from other side of door):* Mr. Trent? *(*TRENT *turns off the lamp. The room is now dark except for the flickering neon sign of the Sunset Motel. Another knock)* Mr. Trent?

TRENT: The door's open.

The door opens. A MAN *stands silhouetted in the bright hallway.*

MAN IN HALLWAY: Mr. Trent?

TRENT: Stay where you are.

MAN IN HALLWAY: Mr. Trent! Apparently, you have not understood the conditions of this meeting . . . The man you are about to see is not supposed to talk to outsiders. By agreeing to do just this for *you,* he places into jeopardy not only his job but his life. For this reason, you were specifically instructed to come alone. Instead, you sent an emissary to check out our hotel. Naturally, the meeting place must now be changed. One more violation and the meeting will be off. We will come for you when we're ready. Your friend has been sent back to New York. *(Leaves)*

TRENT *visible only in the eerie red glow of the neon light.*

TRENT: Poor Stella. And she hates flying, too! (MUSIC: *"Trent's Theme")* I'll tell you, this whole thing, it's not been easy on her . . . Right from the start.

Lights up on STELLA. *The hotel room disappears.*

STELLA *(To audience):* Mike's instructions were simple. He said, "Dollface, I want you to get me every book and article published last year that deals with nuclear weapons." Wow, I thought! Within a week, his desktop looked like the Adirondacks.

TRENT: That's when the trouble began.

Lights up on AUDREY.

AUDREY *(To audience):* About a month after he'd started his research, Stella gave me a call at home. She asked if she could come by. She said it was urgent. I told her to come right over. *(To* STELLA*)* And he's been working?

STELLA: 'Round the clock!

AUDREY: So what's the problem, dear?

STELLA: Well, it's his . . . moaning.

AUDREY: . . . *Moaning?*

STELLA *nods. She holds out a small cassette player. She pushes the Play button. A terrible loud moan is heard.* AUDREY *is aghast.*

TRENT *(To audience):* Actually, I was not aware I was *making* this dreadful noise. I thought I was just reading quietly to myself. I did *hear* the noise, and thought it came from next door. I was in fact about to complain to the landlord, telling him it was hurting my concentration.

AUDREY: Well, this is not right, dear, not right at all. I'll call him in the morning.

TRENT *(To audience):* Which she did. Gave me a real chewing out!

AUDREY: I told him that, in my book, professionals, real professionals, do not sit around moaning. They knuckle down and DO THEIR JOB! No one had *asked* him to be a writer. He agreed.

TRENT: I told her not to worry, I'd figure out the problem. I asked her to arrange a meeting with Stone, and asked if she could be there, too. Frankly, I didn't want to be alone with this guy when I gave him the bad news.

Lights up on STONE *in* AUDREY's *office. He is staring at* TRENT *in cold fury.*

STONE: Well, sir, all I can say is, obviously I've misjudged you! A grave mistake, indeed.

AUDREY *(To* STONE): Now, let's not panic. I'm sure we can work this out. *(To* TRENT) Dear, Mr. Stone has been very generous to you. Don't you think you owe him a little more *time?*

TRENT: I cannot write a play from this material. NO one can write a play from this material! This stuff is INDESCRIBABLE!

AUDREY: Dear, we know the project's difficult. *(To* STONE) I think the research may be getting him down. *(Taking her client aside)* Dear, if you don't deliver a draft to this nice gentleman—doesn't have to be a *good* draft, you understand, just a *draft*—I think this man may not only destroy you financially but possibly have you killed, that's just a feeling I have. Now, what exactly is the problem, please spell it out; perhaps in the *talking,* things will seem easier. *(To* STONE) We're getting there!

TRENT *(With obvious pain):* I have been finding things . . . I did not *expect!*

AUDREY: Dear, that's what research is *about!*

STONE: This is a waste of time. Clearly, Mr. Trent does not have the temperament for serious material.

TRENT: Look, there are certain things playwrights *know!* One of those is what makes a play. This material does not!

AUDREY: Dear, that is the silliest thing you've ever said— *anything* can make a play. You just have to figure out how to *handle* it! I've never seen you like this, really! *(To* STONE) And yet something tells me we're not that far apart.

STONE: If this is not far apart, I am a rabbit!

TRENT *(To* STONE): Look! In every play there is a central character and this central character does not just *want* something; he NEEDS something, needs it so badly if he doesn't *get this thing* he will die . . . not necessarily physically, could be emotionally, spiritually, all right? In fact, dramatically, the worse his potential fate, the better. But! BUT! only up to a point. And that's the problem in this instance. Here, the consequences of failure are so far beyond our imagination, so far beyond anything we have ever experienced, or even *DREAMED,* an audience could not believe, fully believe, what it was watching . . . It will all seem like a lie.

AUDREY: Dear, maybe if you just gave it more *time.*

TRENT: I cannot READ this stuff anymore! I DON'T WANT TO *READ* ABOUT THIS STUFF ANYMORE! "The Prompt and Delayed Effects of Thermonuclear Explosions" is not what I wish to read at night! I am scaring the shit out of my family! My son runs from me in HORROR when he sees me coming. You know why? Because I have become a sentimental goddamn dishrag! I see him walking toward me and I start to weep. I see him playing on the lawn with his dogs and I start to weep. I DON'T WANT TO HAVE TO THINK ABOUT THIS STUFF EVERY DAY! WHAT SORT OF PEOPLE CAN *THINK ABOUT THIS STUFF EVERY DAY?* *(A sudden look of amazement comes over* TRENT*'s face)* . . . I'll work on it.

AUDREY: *What?*

TRENT: I know what to do . . . I'll work on it, I can work on it! I KNOW WHAT TO DO! (AUDREY *stares at him in astonishment, then looks at* STONE *triumphantly. Lights to black on everyone but* TRENT. *To audience)* Through Stone, I arranged to meet with some of the people who think about this stuff every day . . . The ones I asked to meet held opinions that seemed to me to go against all common sense. Anyhow, it was a way in. When there's a mystery, there's at least the possibility of a play. Whatever—it was all I had to go on. Stone said he thought I was doing the right thing. *(Pause)* The first man I talked to, I will call . . . General Wilmer. *(The library of* GENERAL WILMER*'s sumptuous Virginia estate starts to glide in)* He was one of the President's chief advisers on nuclear policy. He had a Ph.D. in physics. *(The* GENERAL *is seated behind an elegant Empire desk. There is an intercom on the desk. He wears casual country-squire clothes)* His house was in Virginia, about an hour's drive from Washington. Usually, he worked at the Pentagon. But this was a Saturday afternoon . . . *(The* GENERAL *lights a pipe)* A lovely autumn day.

GENERAL WILMER: So you want to make a play out of this.

TRENT: Well, that's what I'm hoping.

GENERAL WILMER: Some kind of Strangelove thing?

TRENT: No, I wouldn't think so.

GENERAL WILMER: Good. Because the Strangelove scenario only works if you postulate a Doomsday weapon, and no one contemplates that. To save ourselves by threatening to annihilate ourselves is surely the height of preposterousness!

TRENT: I would think so, yes.

Silence.

GENERAL WILMER: So have you got a plot?

TRENT: Well, no, I'm afraid I don't.

GENERAL WILMER: Don't plays *need* plots?

TRENT: Well, I'm hoping to find one. That's one of the reasons I've come down to Washington.

GENERAL WILMER: *(Merrily):* Not plot in the sense of conspiracy, I trust!

TRENT *(Laughing):* No-no! Plot in the sense of narrative thrust. The thing that makes you ask what happens next. That kind of thing. *(The GENERAL smiles and tamps down the tobacco)* So how long have you known Philip Stone?

GENERAL WILMER: I've never met the man. *(Relights the pipe)*

TRENT: Well, then how did he arrange this meeting?

GENERAL WILMER: Someone else set it up. *(Puffs as an AIDE-DE-CAMP in military uniform enters. He carries a folder. The GENERAL gestures to his desk. The AIDE puts the folder on the desk and leaves)* So. You don't understand why we need more nuclear weapons.

TRENT: Right. It's probably 'cause I'm new at this.

Pause.

GENERAL WILMER: I gave a talk last month at Princeton, and it was on this very issue. And a number of the students started shouting, "Why don't we just *stop* this madness?" And I said, "You know, it's easy to avoid a nuclear war. All you have to do is surrender." *(Grins)* The problem is to find a way to *avoid* nuclear war while preserving the values that we cherish . . . Okay. Don't we have enough to accomplish this right now? Of course we do. Right *now*. But we don't need to deter the Russians now; why would they attack? They'd gain nothing . . . Deterrence comes into play during *crisis*. During crisis, people tend to think in peculiar ways. A successful deterrent says to the Russians, "No matter what, your best case scenario is just no good."

TRENT: But that's where we are right now.

GENERAL WILMER: Of course! But what makes you think we're going to stay where we are? . . . And things may turn better for us, or for them. Either way, it's dangerous. That's because any imbalance at all is dangerous, even if the imbalance is only *imagined*. In this business, it's how you're *perceived* that counts! *(The AIDE enters with a note, which he gives to the GENERAL, then leaves. The GENERAL glances at the note. Crumples it. Puts it in a pocket)* For example, the weaker side starts thinking: Maybe we'd better hit these guys before they get even *stronger*. The stronger side, knowing what the weaker side's thinking, says: Maybe we'd better do what they *think* we're gonna do, even though we don't want to, 'cause otherwise they *might*. In which case, we're done for. So they do. You see? And all this comes about because of one simple, fundamental truth, and it governs everything we do: the guy who goes first goes best.

TRENT: You want more so you can go *first?*

GENERAL WILMER: In a crisis? Absolutely.

Barnard Hughes, John Shea, Linda Hunt

Linda Hunt, John Shea

Barnard Hughes, John Shea

John Shea

TRENT: Well, that is a piece of encouraging news!

GENERAL WILMER: Well, what's the alternative? We say we'd never, under any conditions, go first. And the Russians actually believe us. So *they* go first.

TRENT: Why would they go first if they believe us? I thought you just said they'd go first because they're afraid *we'd* go first!

GENERAL WILMER: Either way.

TRENT: EITHER WAY?

GENERAL WILMER: Well, you certainly can't expect them to believe us *completely.*

TRENT: . . . So it doesn't matter *what* we say.

GENERAL WILMER: In a way, that's true.

TRENT: Maybe we should back up a bit. I think I may have started at too high a level! Why do we need nuclear weapons in the first place?

GENERAL WILMER: To prevent their use.

TRENT: Good. Just what I thought. YET if we suddenly realize we *can't* prevent their use, we'd better hurry up and use them.

GENERAL WILMER: Right.

TRENT: Isn't there some kind of basic contradiction here?

GENERAL WILMER: Absolutely! It's what makes the problem so difficult to solve.

TRENT: Do you enjoy this job?

GENERAL WILMER: Someone's got to do it. *(The intercom buzzes)* Yes?

MAN'S VOICE: The turtle is in Zurich.

GENERAL WILMER *(Stunned):* . . . Zurich? What's it doing in Zurich?

MAN'S VOICE: No one knows. *Should we feed it?*

GENERAL WILMER: . . . Not till we find out what it's doing there. *(Clicks off)*

TRENT: So the turtle is in Zurich! (WILMER *relights his pipe)* Well, I'm GLAD the turtle is in Zurich.

WILMER *smiles at him.*

GENERAL WILMER: No, you're not. *(Pause)* Look. The sole purpose of possessing nuclear weapons . . .

TRENT: . . . is not to win wars but to *prevent* them. I've *got* that. Solid.

GENERAL WILMER: Good. Now. In order to *prevent* a nuclear war, you have to be able to *fight* a nuclear war at *all levels,* even though they're probably unwinnable and unfightable. You understand, this doesn't mean you want to. Doesn't even mean you *will.* That's because, for the purpose of deterrence, a bluff taken seriously is far more helpful than a serious threat taken as a bluff. What we're talking about now is credibility. Okay? . . . To this end, what your opponent *thinks* you'll do is much more important than what you *actually* will do. *(Buzzer sounds. He flicks the intercom)* I'm sorry, not now. *(Clicks off)* For example, for the purpose of deterrence, it's a good idea to tell the Russians that if they move into Western Europe—*(Buzzer sounds. He flicks the intercom)* What?

LITTLE BOY'S VOICE: Dad?

GENERAL WILMER: Dear. Not now. All right? *(Clicks off)*—
that if they move into Western Europe we will use nuclear
weapons to stop their advance. No ambiguity there: you make
this move, we make *this* move. However! Should deterrence
fail, it would seem wiser not to use our nuclear weapons at all,
the reason being that once we've gone nuclear, the likelihood
of Soviet nuclear retaliation is overwhelming. *(Enter* AIDE *with
note. He hands it to* WILMER. WILMER *keeps talking)* What's
more, the probability is that it would escalate. What this
means is that instead of Western Europe being overrun by the
Soviets—*(He glances at the note)*—a thing we certainly don't
want! *(To the* AIDE) Have his mother take care of it. *(Exit the*
AIDE)—Western Europe, *and* the United States, AND the Soviet Union would quickly and effectively cease to exist. In fact,
according to our latest figures, so probably would the entire
world. *(Buzzer sounds. He flicks it. With annoyance)* Yes?

WOMAN'S VOICE: This is for *you* to handle, dear.

GENERAL WILMER: I'll take care of it later. *(Clicks off)* Okay,
so here we are, then, with two policies, one overt—you move
here and we will strike; the second, *covert*—we may choose not
to do any such thing. The Soviets, who know it makes no *sense*
for us to strike with nuclear weapons if they move in, nonethe-
less are deterred from moving in because it's *just possible* we
might be *crazy* enough to do it. *Now.* What this means is that,
for every level of engagement, we must possess a credible response, even if this response is quite incredible on its surface.
This is one of the reasons it's important for our President,
whoever he is, to every so often say something that sounds a
bit insane. *(Pause)* Fear, you see. That's the great deterrent
. . . Don't want to do too much to reduce the fear. By the
way, that's the problem with a nuclear freeze: to the extent
that it makes people feel safer, it raises the chances of war. You
look shocked. I'll tell you something shocking—I think things
are going just fine. And you should relax. We really *do* know

what we're doing. Take a look. In the past forty years, have we had a nuclear war? No. Why? . . . Nuclear weapons. The fact is, nuclear weapons not only prevent *nuclear* war, they prevent *all* war . . . And I think they just may be the best damned thing that's ever happened to us. Really do!

Beat. Blackout on everything but TRENT.

MUSIC: *"Trent's Theme."* TRENT *walks downstage to the audience.*

TRENT *(To audience):* My conversation with General Wilmer had left me in a quandary: I didn't know whether to laugh or cry. I was on the verge of doing both when the general gave me a call.

Lights up on WILMER.

GENERAL WILMER: I've been thinking. Maybe you should meet a man named Stanley Berent. If you like, I can set it up.

Lights off on WILMER.

TRENT *(To audience):* I'd come across Berent's name in my research. He was a Russian scholar, connected to Georgetown University, and a real hard-liner, particularly where the Soviet Union was concerned. *(Japanese koto music heard)* We met at a small Japanese restaurant I assume he frequented out of war guilt. We sat on tatami mats, cross-legged, which made the experience even more excruciating. An inescapable feeling of unreality began to hang over all of this.

The restaurant has slid into view during the above.

BERENT *(Eastern European accent):* No, I agree with you completely—our present nuclear policy does not make sense, not at all!

TRENT *(To audience):* Why had the general sent me to *this* man?

BERENT: What we must do—very simple: we must stop regarding nuclear war as some kind of goddamn inevitable holocaust . . . and start looking at it as a goddamn WAR!

TRENT: . . . What?

BERENT: We have to learn how to wage nuclear war *rationally.*

TRENT: *What?*

BERENT: Rationally. We have got to learn how to wage nuclear war *rationally.* I'm sorry—*sake?*

TRENT: Uhhhhh, thank you.

BERENT: You see, even though a strong case can be made for the fact that nuclear war is essentially an act of insane desperation, and therefore fundamentally irrational, this doesn't mean that once you're in the thing you shouldn't do it *right!*

TRENT: I see. *(Pause)* Of course, this would seem to suggest you think it's possible to *win* a nuclear war.

BERENT: No-no! *Limited* nuclear war. No one can win an all-out nuclear war. Unless, of course, the other side decides not to hit back, and one could never count on that, ALTHOUGH, I must say—*(Gives a brief, sharp command to a* WAITRESS *in fluent Japanese)*—although, I must say, in all the scenarios I've seen, the side that hits first definitely comes out best. So if push comes to shove, you do go first, no question of it, particularly if you employ what we call a controlled counterforce strike with restraint. In effect, you hit everything but your opponent's cities.

TRENT: That's the restraint part.

BERENT: Right. His cities are held hostage. And what you—
I'm sorry! Chopsticks?

TRENT: Yes, chopsticks.

BERENT: And what you do is, you tell him you'll demolish
them if he doesn't capitulate. Now, this is actually quite rea-
sonable, *if,* big if, *big* if, IF you have an adequate civil-defense
system. That way, even if the Russians strike back, you should
be able to absorb the blow and still have enough left to strike
back at *them.* And this time just wipe them out. This is what I
mean when I talk about credibility. What I have just described
to you is a CREDIBLE offensive and defensive nuclear strategy. What we have now, forgive my French, is diddly-shit. *(To
the* WAITRESS, *a short command in Japanese, at which she nods
and leaves. To* TRENT*)* You don't speak Japanese, I take it.

TRENT: No. Why? Are you passing secrets?

BERENT *(Laughing):* Secrets? I'm not privy to any secrets.
Ah, thank you. *(A* WAITER *delivers a noddle dish)* Now. Do I
really know how to fight a limited nuclear war? Not at all. No
one does. No one's *fought* one. And yet if we're not prepared,
we're in the soup. Okay. What do I propose?

TRENT: You're not eating.

BERENT: I'm not hungry. What do I propose. I propose we
send a clear signal to the Russians, and this signal says: You
fuck around with us, we're gonna fuck around with you! This
is the sort of talk the Russians understand. How do we do this?
First, we build the MX, the Trident 2, the Pershing II, and the
Cruise. Why do I want these things? Because they have the
ability to take out hardened targets. If we get into a major

crisis with these people, I want the ability to disarm them to the greatest extent possible.

TRENT: *Disarm?*

BERENT: Remove. Surgically remove. As much of their military capability as is possible.

TRENT: That's called a first strike, I believe.

BERENT: Oh, no.

TRENT: It's *not?*

BERENT: No.

Pause.

TRENT: Why?

BERENT: Because the connotation is *aggressive.* This is a *defensive* act.

TRENT: I see . . . Out of curiosity, what do you call it?

BERENT: Anticipatory retaliation.

TRENT: Ah!

BERENT: Some prefer "preemptive strike," but that can get cumbersome. Because, if you sense they're about to preempt *you,* then what you have to do is *pre*-preempt them.

TRENT *(Getting into the spirit now):* And of course if they should somehow become *aware* that you've discovered their *plans* to preempt, and are about to *pre*-preempt, they'll have to start discussing a *pre*-pre-preemptive strike. And one can obviously just get lost in this kind of talk.

BERENT: That's right. Anticipatory retaliation simply covers everything! Unfortunately, we can't even begin to consider this if we don't have the proper weapons.

TRENT: And we don't have them now?

BERENT: No, sir, we do not.

TRENT: I realize you're going to lose all respect for me. But isn't is possible we'd be better off *not* getting these things?

BERENT: Of course! . . . If the Russians didn't have them.

TRENT: They *have* them?

BERENT: They're *getting* them.

TRENT: WHERE DOES THIS ALL END?

BERENT: When each of us is secure.

TRENT: Well, that's fair enough.

BERENT: Unfortunately, we're not even close . . . To be secure, the United States must possess a credible nuclear-war fighting policy. Now, what might such a policy be?

TRENT: Got me.

BERENT: In a war, what do you think the Russian command would least like to lose?

TRENT: I would say, offhand, Russia.

BERENT: Short of that.

TRENT: Half of Russia?

BERENT: Short of *that.*

TRENT: A third of Russia.

BERENT: Wrong approach. The point is to avoid killing civilians needlessly. Now, come on, think. In a war, outside of its population, what can the Soviet leaders least afford to lose?

TRENT: . . . I don't know.

BERENT: Oh, come on!

TRENT: No, really, I don't know.

BERENT: ThemSELVES!

TRENT: Themselves?

BERENT: Of course! Without a Kremlin, without leadership— you know what Russia's got? It's got shit, that's what it's got!

TRENT: So how do we get rid of their leaders?

BERENT: Well, we know where they are. And we bomb them.

TRENT: . . . Surely they're not just going to sit there and *wait!*

BERENT: No-no! They're going to hide. That's expected.

TRENT: I would think Russia has a lot of hiding places.

BERENT: Of course. And we know where they are. And we target them.

TRENT: Sounds to me like you're about to wipe out all of Russia.

BERENT: Well, that's certainly not what we *intend.*

TRENT: It's just a side effect, you mean.

BERENT: Correct.

TRENT: And this wouldn't piss them off?

BERENT: Piss *who* off?

TRENT: The Russians who are left. I see! They're all *gone.*

BERENT: That's right.

TRENT: Listen. Question. Let's say we've successfully wiped out their leaders, somehow some of their population still exist, and we decide we want to stop this thing. With *whom* do we negotiate?

BERENT: Well, that is a genuine problem.

TRENT: Listen, this is just off the top of my head. Don't you think it might be a good idea to try really very seriously to *negotiate* something with these fellas *now?*

BERENT: Of course! That would be *wonderful!* And yet, if history shows anything, it shows that the Soviet Union cannot be trusted to keep the terms of a treaty!

TRENT: Hold it! Hold it, hold it! Are you trying to tell me we shouldn't enter into treaties with these guys till we're convinced they can be TRUSTED?

BERENT: That's correct.

TRENT: If we knew they could be trusted, why would we need TREATIES? *SAYONARA!* (BERENT *stares at him in astonishment. To audience)* I could barely contain my excitement!

(Rises as BERENT *and the restaurant fade from view)* I called Stone at the first pay phone I could find. *(Lights up on* STONE. *He is in a room next to a wing chair, its back to us)* Okay, I've got it!

STONE *(Trace of nervousness in his voice):* Got what, sir?

TRENT: The answer. The mystery is solved. I've discovered why we're doomed.

STONE: Really. And why is that?

TRENT: We're in the hands of assholes! *(Silence)* . . . Hello?

STONE *(Sotto voce):* I'm afraid I cannot speak right now.

TRENT: Why?

The lights have come up enough to reveal that there is a man sitting in the wing chair—we see only his legs. The man appears to be smoking, for smoke curls upward from the chair.

STONE: Sir, I can only tell you, if you persist in believing these men you've met are not smart, or not . . . *(In a whisper)* dangerous . . . *(Back to his normal voice)* . . . you are gravely mistaken. I can say no more, not now.

STONE *hangs up. Turns back to his mysterious companion. Lights to black on them both.*

TRENT *(To audience):* There are times you want to chuck it all. This wasn't one. I was on to something here, no question. I decided to check out the guys they call war-gamers, the guys who *play* with these war scenarios. I called General Wilmer and asked if he could arrange it—things had gone so well with the last meeting he'd set up! He said he would. Gladly. And he did. *(Lights up on* JIM *and* PETE) I will call them Jim and Pete. *(We are in* JIM*'s kitchen)* Both were connected with the Harley

Corporation, a government think tank in nearby Virginia. (PETE *and* JIM *are preparing a meal—tiny birds stuffed, seasoned, wrapped in gauze, to be cooked in a microwave)* But the place was off-limits to plain ol' folk like me, so they very graciously invited me to Jim's house, though perhaps it was Pete's, I was never altogether sure—*one* of theirs. For a meal in my honor. Why had they gone to all this trouble for me? Something was very odd.

JIM *(While working at the meal):* So you talked with Stanley Berent!

PETE *(Also while working at the meal):* Bet *that* was fun!

TRENT: He poked a lot of holes in our deterrence strategy.

JIM: I'm sure he was right, it's not hard to do.

They work in tandem on the meal; lots of coordinated teamwork.

PETE: There's a curious paradox built into deterrence strategy, and no one has a *clue* how to get around it. The paradox is this: Deterrence is dependent upon strength—well, that's obvious; the stronger your nuclear arsenal, the more the other side's deterred. *However,* should deterrence *fail* for any reason, your strength *instantly* becomes your greatest liability, *inviting* attack *instead* of preventing it.

JIM: HOIST on your own petard!

PETE: And *that* is where all these crazy scenarios come in in which war breaks out PRECISELY because *no one* WANTS it to! Really! I'm not kidding. This business is *filled* with paradox! Here, I'll run one by you.

JIM: I think, before you do, we should point out it isn't *easy* starting a nuclear war.

PETE: Right! Sorry. Getting carried away.

JIM: In fact, we can run scenario after scenario—the Persian Gulf is the most popular.

PETE: That's the hot spot!

JIM: People just will not go nuclear.

PETE: Right! And at first it absolutely drove us up the wall! Here we had all these tests designed to see what happens when people go nuclear?

JIM: And no one would do it!

PETE: To the man, they just refused to believe there wasn't some other way to resolve the crisis!

JIM: Well, the military started freaking out. They figured all those guys down in the silos?—maybe they won't push the button when they're told.

PETE: Real freak-out scene.

JIM: The whole Pentagon—

PETE: They just went bananas! *Total* banana scene.

JIM: Some general called me up. He said, "You incompetent jackass, what the hell kind of scenario are you *giving* these guys?" I said, "We're giving 'em every scenario we can think of, SIR! No one'll push the button, SIR!" You know what he said?

PETE: Get this!—"Don't tell 'em it's the button!"

JIM: "Really!" we said. "Then what good's the test?"

PETE: Anyway, happy ending.

JIM: Finally we solved it.

PETE: *You* solved it.

JIM: *I* solved it, *you* solved it, what's it matter? We *solved* the thing!

PETE: What a bitch!

JIM: People think it's *easy* starting a nuclear war?

PETE: Hey! Let 'em try!

TRENT: Okay, I'll bite: how *do* you start a nuclear war?

JIM: Well, *first* you have to assume that a nuclear war is the *last* thing either side wants.

PETE: Right! That's the key! Who would've thought it! Jim?

JIM: Okay. Let's say we're in a confrontation situation where we and the Soviets are facing down in the Middle East: let's say, Iran. Big Soviet pour-down. Let's further say we're losing conventionally on the ground—

PETE: Not hard to believe—

JIM: —and the President decides he wants the option of using nuclear weapons in the area, so he moves them in.

PETE: Mind you, he doesn't want to *use* them now.

JIM: Right! Absolutely not! Last thing he wants!

PETE: He's just hoping, by showing strength, the Soviets will rethink their position and pull back.

JIM: In other words, it's a *bluff.*

PETE: Right, good ol' poker bluff!

JIM: And, by the way, probably the proper move to make.

PETE: Now, at the *same* time we ask our NATO allies to join us in raising the military alert level in Europe. Why? We want to tie the Soviet forces down that are in Eastern Europe.

JIM: Again, absolutely the right move.

PETE: So far, the President's batting a thousand. No appeasement here. Yet not too strong, nothing precipitous.

JIM: Okay. The Soviets now go to a higher level of readiness themselves. Why? They want to tie *our* forces down so *we* don't shift 'em to the Middle East.

PETE: Now we start to move nuclear weapons out of storage! *(Mimics the sound of a trumpet)*

JIM: Okay, now let's suppose the Soviets, in the heat of this crisis, *misinterpret* the moves we've made, and believe that in fact we're about to *launch* these weapons! Not a farfetched supposition!

PETE: Particularly, given their tendency to paranoia!

JIM: Right!

PETE: Okay. Now, at *this* point the issue for them is *not* do they want to be *in* a war.

JIM: They're already *in* a war in the Middle East!

PETE: Right. The issue isn't even do they want to launch a nuclear attack against the West.

JIM: That's because they know they'll HAVE to if the West attacks *them!*

PETE: You see?

JIM: *The only issue—*

PETE: Absolutely ONLY issue—

JIM: —is do they want to go *first* and *preempt* this attack?

PETE: Or wait it out—

JIM: —and go second.

PETE: Now, they recognize, just as much as we . . .

JIM: . . . that going *first—*

PETE: —is going *best.*

JIM: Right!

PETE: And by a shocking margin, too. No scenario *ever* shows ANYTHING else! I mean, these notions of our riding out a nuclear attack and then launching again, without substantial loss of capability—well, it's nonsense.

JIM: By the way, you have to posit here that events are moving rapidly. A short time frame is crucial to this scenario. No time to sit back and say, "Hey! wait, why would he want to shoot at me? I know he's in trouble, but he isn't crazy!" No. He doesn't have *time* to think things out. He's got to make a move! Okay, What's he do? (PETE *makes the gesture and sound of a missile taking off*) He shoots. Now, are we saying it's a likely thing? No. But, from the Soviet perspective, they HAVE to shoot. Under these conditions, holding back is clearly wrong, politically and militarily.

PETE: And *that*—

JIM: —is how a nuclear war begins.

PETE: Not out of anger.

JIM: Or greed.

PETE: But *fear!*

JIM: With neither side *wanting* to.

PETE: Yet each side *having* to.

JIM: 'Cause the other guy thinks they're *going* to.

PETE: So they'd better.

PETE and JIM *(Together, à la W. C. Fields):* HOIST ON OUR OWN PETARD!

JIM: By the way, where *is* the petard?

PETE *(Tossing a jar of mustard):* Petard!

JIM *(Catching it):* Petard!

PETE and JIM *(Together, à la W. C. Fields):* Ahhhh, yes!

TRENT: You guys are a scream.

JIM: Actually—should we tell him?

PETE: Sure.

JIM: Actually, over at the center, we all try to scream at least once a day.

PETE: Usually it happens in the cafeteria.

JIM: Someone on the staff will stand up and shout "SCREAMIN' TIME!" And everyone just, you know . . . *(Gives a choked comic scream)*

PETE: It's a ritual we only do when no one from the Pentagon's around.

JIM: We did it once when some honcho military brass were there.

PETE: *Freaked them out!*

JIM: Within minutes we had lost I don't know *how* many grants! *(Laughs)*

PETE: So, anyway, now we're pretty choosy 'bout who we scream in front of.

JIM: I'll tell you . . . I sometimes think, if it really happens, and we all, you know . . . *(Makes the sound and gesture of a giant explosion)* . . . and by the way, the whole thing *could* be over! No matter what anybody says, no one knows *what* happens to the ozone layer in a nuclear war. Really! No idea! *(Laughs)* Okay, so I sometimes think, now it's all over, and we're all up there in the big debriefing space in the sky, and the Good Lord decides to hold a symposium 'cause he's curious: how did this thing happen? And everybody says, "Hey, don't look at me, I didn't wanna do it!" The end result being that everyone realizes *no* one wanted to do it! But there was suddenly no choice. Or no choice they could *see.* And the symposium gets nowhere.

TRENT: How do we get out of this?

PETE: Well, you try like hell to not get *into* these kinds of conflicts!

JIM: Obviously, sometimes it can't be helped.

TRENT: This is not pleasant news.

PETE *(Putting the birds into the microwave):* On the other hand, let's not exaggerate. Things are not that bad, maybe we *shouldn't* get out of it. *(With a laugh, to* JIM) Would you not love to have a snapshot of this man's expression?

JIM *mimes taking a snapshot of* TRENT.

TRENT: So you mean we're just supposed to sit around, twiddle our thumbs, and WAIT?

PETE: Well . . .

JIM: Sometimes . . . there's really not an awful lot you *can* do.

PETE: Except *hold on.*

JIM: And hope for some kind of discontinuity.

PETE: Right.

TRENT: Ah! Discontinuity! What the hell is that?

PETE: It's an event . . . by definition unpredictable, which causes a sudden and radical shift in the general mode of thinking.

JIM: Sadat's going to Jerusalem is the prime example.

PETE: Sadat looked down the road and saw nuclear weapons in Cairo and Alexandria in maybe five, ten years, and he just didn't like what he saw.

JIM: So he decided he was gonna do something about it.

PETE: And what he decided to do no one, I mean *no* one, anticipated.

JIM: And it changed the whole ball game.

PETE: *Just like that!*

JIM: And THAT—

PETE: —is a discontinuity.

TRENT: Okay! all right! . . . any candidates?

PETE: Well, I'd say the best we've come up with so *far* is . . . *(Looks to* JIM *for help)*

JIM *(To* PETE*):* Extraterrestrial?

PETE: Yah. *(To* TRENT*)* Extraterrestrial.

TRENT *(Stunned):* You mean, like E.T. comes down?

PETE: You got it!

TRENT: Jesus Christ!

JIM: That's another!

TRENT: You guys are a riot!

JIM: Hey! In this business? Important to keep smiling.

TRENT: No, I can see that. Listen, have you guys given any real thought to, you know, touring the country? Nightclubs, things like that?

PETE: Oh, sure, it's occurred to us.

TRENT: I'm sure it has.

JIM: People are very interested in this nuclear issue.

PETE: And we're right there at the dirty heart of it!

TRENT: Good. Listen, while we're on the subject of humor, what's your attitude toward doom?

PETE: . . . *Doom?*

PETE *looks at* JIM. JIM *looks at* PETE.

JIM: It's just no solution.

PETE: No. No solution.

TRENT: I'm being serious!

PETE and JIM *(Together):* So are we! *(They smile at* TRENT)

Blackout on JIM *and* PETE. TRENT *turns to the audience.* MU-SIC: *"Trent's Theme."*

TRENT: Okay. Even with *my* lousy sinuses, I could tell something wasn't smelling right. I figured it was *my* fault. What've I missed? I decided to retrace my steps. (TRENT*'s office has begun to reappear)* The next day I was back in my office in Stamford, going through all my notes, when Stella came in with a rather large package.

Enter STELLA *pushing a huge flat object wrapped in plain brown paper.*

STELLA: Boy, is this big!

On the wrapper, crayoned in enormous black letters, are these words:

MICHAEL TRENT—PLAYWRIGHT
and
DETECTIVE

TRENT: Hey, dollface, what gives?

STELLA: I dunno. I found it in the hallway. Someone left it outside your door. I had t' bring it in, 'cause otherwise I couldn't get out. *(Starts to unwrap it)*

TRENT: *(To audience):* It had no return address.

Inside the package is an oversized, framed photograph. This is the photograph:

See Back Endpaper

TRENT *and* STELLA *stare at it in silence.*

STELLA: Hey, Mike, how do ya *build* a box like that?

TRENT: I dunno.

STELLA: Hey! Maybe there's instructions in the back. *(Checks in back)* Mikey! Look! . . . A card.

STELLA *hands the small white card to* TRENT. TRENT, *not needing to read, moves toward the audience. As he does,* STELLA, *the box, and the office disappear into the dark.*

TRENT *(To audience):* The card said, "If you want help with your quest, be in Washington tomorrow night, ten o'clock." And it was signed "The Shadow." *(There is the sound of a knock from the darkness behind him.* TRENT *turns toward the sound)* It's open!

The door of his hotel room has appeared. It opens. The MAN *who appeared earlier is seen, silhouetted against a dazzlingly bright white hallway light.*

MAN IN HALLWAY: We're ready, Mr. Trent.

TRENT: Right! *(Blackout except for a pin-spot of light on* TRENT*)* I am led down the backstairs to a car—an old Ford wagon. In the rear seat are two men. I get in. No one says a word to me. And the car pulls out . . . Fog moves in off the Potomac . . . We are heading toward the center of the capital, that much I can tell. We move at a crawl. Even the road is scarcely visible. *(Pause)* And then . . . the sky begins to *glow.* A dazzling milky phosphorescence! I have never seen anything like this in my life! And then I hear *music. (Music dimly heard)* . . . *Band* music. *(So it is)* And then I see the *source* of this strange light! *(Music louder)* We approach the Jefferson Memorial. On the grounds surrounding it are rows upon rows of giant klieg lights! The lawn—what I can see of it—is packed. Obviously, it's a concert of some sort. We pass near a clearing in the fog, and I see that in the crowd are many men in military uniforms! . . . The car stops. I can see a sign but can't make out what it says. The people who have brought me here tell me to get out. "But how will I recognize The Shadow?" I say. "Don't worry," they say. "But where should I walk?" "Wherever you wish." So I get out and the car drives off. *(Pause)* I head for the sign. The sign says: U.S. Marine Corps Band. *(Music louder)* Well, I don't like crowds in the best of times, and this is terrible! So I decide to go toward the Memorial, which looms through the fog like a spectral white mushroom. *(The interior of the Jefferson Memorial begins to form around him)* The rotunda is empty. I look down through the fog and can see . . . almost no one. *(Jefferson's statue can be discerned only in shape. The same for the surrounding columns)* And then I hear . . .

Footsteps suddenly moving toward him. Then they stop on the far side of a shimmering shaft of light caused by the klieg lights' piercing the fog. All we can see of this MAN *are the bottoms of his legs.*

MAN'S VOICE: Mr. Trent?

TRENT: And I recognize the voice!

The MAN *walks toward* TRENT, *through the eerie light. The first feature we see is that he is in uniform. But we can't yet make out his face. And then he moves forward, into a better light. It is* GENERAL WILMER. *He smiles.*

GENERAL WILMER *(Warmly):* Shall we talk?

Beat. Blackout.

Curtain

The Discovery

Lights up on TRENT *in his trench coat.*

TRENT: Okay. I have proceeded systematically, I have followed my nose and have found the piece of the puzzle I was looking for. Unfortunately, instead of the puzzle being solved, the puzzle has expanded . . . I am a man who knows too much . . . and not enough. *Why me? Why has Stone picked me? (The cozy living room of* TRENT*'s house in Connecticut slides into view. Through rear windows, open, with curtains fluttering in a gentle spring breeze, we can see trees and a meadow)* By the way, this is my house in Connecticut—my beloved retreat to which I have retreated. Fat chance! About an hour ago, Stone called to say he was coming out to see how I'm doing. *How I'm doing!* . . . All right, the truth: I have told him the meeting with The Shadow was canceled. Actually, I didn't have the nerve to tell him this directly, I left a message. I've told the same thing to my agent and my wife. I need time to think things through! It's not an easy racket, writing plays; stay out of it!

ALEX *(Offstage):* DAD!

TRENT: That's my son. He's eleven.

BOY'S VOICE: I think your producer's here!

TRENT: Great. Here it goes.

BOY'S VOICE: Should I tell Mom to let him in?

TRENT: No-no! Let him find his own way in! *(To audience)* My wife is on the patio, in a chaise, reading Yeats. That's what life's like here in the country. Now, if things go well today— and at this point I've no idea just how that's possible—you won't be meeting either my wife *or* my son; as I said earlier, I don't want them involved in this!

STONE: TRENT!

TRENT: The Call of the Wild! *(To* STONE) I'M IN THE LIV-ING ROOM, PHIL! *(To audience)* What you are about to see is scrambling of the highest order! (TRENT *removes his trench coat. Enter* STONE) Phil! (STONE *stops and turns his gaze on* TRENT. *He stares at* TRENT *closely. Then, after a moment,* STONE *grins)* Well, I'm glad to see you're happy!

STONE *walks slowly over to* TRENT *and rests his hands on* TRENT's *shoulders.* TRENT *stares back, terrified.* STONE *continues to grin.*

STONE: I haven't seen you in such a long time!

TRENT: That's right! About . . . a month, I guess—maybe . . . more.

STONE: Why was the meeting canceled?

TRENT: Oh! With, uhh, The Shadow? I don't know, they didn't say. Security, I suspect. I'm waiting now to see when it will be rescheduled.

STONE: What makes you think it will be rescheduled?

TRENT: Well, that's what they said.

STONE: And yet, for some reason, they neglected to tell you why it was canceled.

TRENT: No-no, uh, *security!* . . . I mean they, you know, *said* that. Said it. "Too risky for him to meet with you tonight" —that's what they said.

Enter ANN, TRENT's *wife. She is in her sixth month of pregnancy.*

ANN: Dear, Audrey has arrived.

TRENT: What?

ANN *(Going toward* STONE*):* Hi! I'm Ann Trent.

TRENT: Ann! Out! Get out!

ANN: *What?*

He rushes toward her.

TRENT *(Sotto voce):* Get out of here! Go! I'll tell you about it later. I don't want you involved in this! Out, get out! *(Leads/ pushes/coaxes her out of the room as* AUDREY *enters)* Audrey!

STONE: I was not aware you were joining us today!

AUDREY: No. Nor was my client. Dear, I need to speak to you alone.

TRENT *(Startled):* Of course.

AUDREY: Mr. Stone, would you mind very much if my client and I went into—

STONE: No, please, dear lady, you stay here, I can use the time to look around the house. I *love* country houses! And this is such a charming one. *(Exits)*

TRENT *stares after him, perplexed.*

TRENT: Well, he's the weirdest man I've ever met!

AUDREY: Dear, I'm afraid I have some extremely bad news for you.

TRENT: Oh!

AUDREY: Could I have a drink?

TRENT: Uhhhh, right. Ummmm—

AUDREY: *Martini.*

TRENT: With an *olive!*

AUDREY: No, dear. Lemon twist.

TRENT: Right, of course. *(Heading for the bar)* So what's the, uh, bad news?

AUDREY: Well. It seems, dear, that your producer has instituted legal action against you.

TRENT: *What?*

AUDREY: He is bringing suit against you, dear. For fraud and breach of contract.

TRENT: WHAT?

AUDREY: Sssh. Dear. Please.

TRENT: *Why?*

AUDREY: I'm not sure.

TRENT: Well, how much is he suing me for? I mean, is it the retainer, the advance?

AUDREY: I'm afraid it's a bit more than that.

TRENT: How can it be for more, that's all I made!

AUDREY: The suit is for fifteen million dollars.

TRENT: Fifteen million DOLLARS?

AUDREY: Yes, dear, dollars.

TRENT: But that makes no SENSE!

AUDREY: I know.

TRENT: Maybe it's not dollars! Maybe it's zlotys!

AUDREY: No, dear, dollars, Yankee dollars.

TRENT: WHAT'S HE THINK I'VE *GOT?*

AUDREY: Well . . . it's not worth a *great* deal . . . but you've got this house.

TRENT *(Staring in direction that* STONE *went):* Oh, my God!

AUDREY: Perhaps if you turned in your *script!*

TRENT: Oh, come on, Audrey! No one sues a playwright for fifteen million dollars because he's a few weeks late delivering a script! I mean, what's he hope to gain? A house? He doesn't need another house!

STONE *(Who has entered, unnoticed):* It's not the house that interests me . . . It's your *ruination. (They turn to him, astonished)* And I expect your legal fees alone should accomplish that. You look surprised; that surprises me. Did you really think I'd allow your treachery to go unchallenged?

TRENT: What are you talking about?

STONE: Sir, please, the time for innocence is past.

AUDREY: *What* treachery?

STONE: Evidence suggests, madam, that your client has in fact found what he set *out* to find.

TRENT: That's not TRUE!

STONE: And I believe otherwise.

AUDREY: Michael, have you lied to Mr. Stone?

TRENT: Not at all.

AUDREY: You owe my client an apology.

STONE: Tell this lady what you've done.

TRENT: *I don't know WHAT you are TALKING about.*

STONE: Does the name "The Shadow" ring a bell?

TRENT: The meeting was called OFF!

STONE: AND THAT, SIR, IS A LIE!

AUDREY: Mr. Stone, forgive me. If my client says the meeting was called off, the meeting was called off.

STONE: I disagree.

AUDREY: Michael?

TRENT: It was called off.

AUDREY: The matter's closed.

STONE: THIS MAN HAS VIOLATED THE TERMS OF OUR AGREEMENT!

AUDREY: Mr. Stone!

TRENT: Audrey.

AUDREY: Dear, let me handle this! *(To* STONE*)* I believe the time has come, sir, for you to leave.

STONE *(To* TRENT*):* Tell her what you've done.

AUDREY: Is there something wrong, sir, with your ears?

TRENT: Audrey.

AUDREY: I SAID STAY OUT OF THIS! I CAN HANDLE THIS! *(To* STONE*)* Mr. Stone, if my client says the meeting was called off, it was called off. My clients do not lie to me.

TRENT *(Weakly):* Audrey, please.

AUDREY: DEAR, STAY OUT OF THIS! *(To* STONE*)* The matter's therefore closed. Except, sir, for your appalling lack of manners. Where, may I ask, were you brought up?

TRENT: I LIED!!!! *(She turns to him as if struck)* I lied, I lied! I'm sorry! *(He holds his head in his hands and fights tears. She does not know what to do, where to turn. She turns to* STONE*)*

AUDREY *(To* STONE*):* Would you . . . be so kind . . .

STONE: A drink?

AUDREY: Yes, please, some . . . water would be nice, I think. *(To* TRENT) Why? Don't you trust me?

TRENT: Of course I trust you! This has nothing to do with trust! I just had no idea what to say. I haven't even told Ann! I've told no one!

AUDREY *(Taking the glass from* STONE): I owe you an apology.

STONE: Not at all.

AUDREY *(To* TRENT): I don't understand what's happening.

TRENT *(To* STONE, *angrily):* Did you set the meeting up? (STONE *shakes his head no)* Then how do you know it happened?

STONE: I've had you followed, sir. Ever since you accepted this job.

TRENT: Great!

STONE: I should add, in all this time my emissaries have never actually seen you *writing*.

TRENT: What do you think, I write in the *street?* I write in my OFFICE!

STONE: Good! Then you can show me some pages.

TRENT: *Pages?*

STONE: Sir, doom approaches, I need pages.

TRENT: ANYONE CAN WRITE PAGES!

STONE: I ask only to see yours.

TRENT: Well, I never show pages till I'm done. Audrey can confirm this. Audrey, are you all right? *(She nods)* Anyhow, the important thing isn't pages, the important thing is *concept!* CONCEPT is what we should be talking about! Without a concept, a play is nothing.

STONE: Sir, a play may be nothing without a concept—without pages, it is even less.

TRENT: Who said that? Aristotle, I believe.

AUDREY *(Sotto voce):* Dear, this man is *suing* you!

TRENT: Okay, fine, you want pages? I'll give you pages! I've got pages *here—(Runs to a drawer, opens it)*—and in here— *(Opens another drawer)*—pages everywhere! You want pages? Here! Pages! *(Starts flinging the pages into the air.* STONE *looks down at them)*

STONE: These are not pages from a play!

TRENT: Right! For that, you need a CONCEPT!

AUDREY: *Michael.*

TRENT *(To* AUDREY, *sotto voce):* I'm okay, I know what I'm doing. Really. *(To* STONE) Now, do you want to hear what my concept is? Because I will tell you. Gladly. Because this is a concept I am wild about! And it took a long time finding. In fact, I only found it today. But well worth the waiting, because this concept means this play will be *fun.*

STONE: *What?*

TRENT: Fun! Fun to write, fun to look at.

AUDREY: Dear, are we talking about the same play?

TRENT: Of course! The play that deals with doom! Going to be fun! So you want to hear what this concept is? Okay, here it is . . . *(Very long pause, during which time he takes out a ciga- rette and hopes that a concept will come. The lighting of the cigarette, in a kind of Philip Marlowe way, seems to do the trick. A look of astonishment comes over his face, which he masks from the others)* The playwright . . . is conceived . . . as being very much like a *detective. (To* AUDREY) Wha'd'ya think?

STONE: *What* playwright?

TRENT: The playwright who's at the CENTER of this play!

STONE: What's a playwright doing in this play?

TRENT: He's in this play because he is the only reality I can hang on to here! And this playwright is sent on a *strannnnge* mission by a man, I would say quite like *you,* a kindly man, a man who would surely never, for example, sue anyone. And this playwright *respects* this man because this playwright is without doubt the very salt of the earth! Though possibly with some knowledge of evil—I still haven't figured that one out, I may have to come back to you for that, I'm nowhere on that so far, that's the truth, I just can't remember where we met. *(Silence)* Okay, so this playwright, down he goes to Washing- ton, figuring if this mystery can be solved anywhere, there's the spot.

AUDREY: Dear, what happened down in Washington?

TRENT: The case took a turn for the worse, all right? I didn't think it possible.

AUDREY: Michael, *please!*

TRENT: I DO NOT BELIEVE WHAT THE SHADOW TOLD ME, OKAY? And there you are. Now, what am I to do with that?

Enter ANN TRENT, *carrying a tea tray.*

ANN: Tea time!

TRENT *(Angry, sotto voce):* Ann, I asked you specifically—

ANN: Dear, I am not coming to sit in on your meeting, this is *your* meeting, not mine. *(To* AUDREY *and* STONE*)* I just thought you might all like some iced tea. The mint is from the garden. *(To* TRENT, *sotto voce)* I was being *nice.* You might try the same. *(She sets the tray down and leaves. Silence)*

STONE: When is your wife due?

TRENT: Uh, due where? . . . Oh! Uhhh, she's, let's see, in her sixth month, so in four, I mean three. Unless doom strikes first, of course. I'm sorry, I'm just very edgy today.

ANN *comes back in, holding the sugar bowl. She comes face to face with a glowering* TRENT. *She puts the bowl down on the floor.*

ANN: The sugar.

She tiptoes back out.

STONE: She's very graceful, your wife.

TRENT: Yes. *(Silence)* Look, you want to know what happened down in Washington? You show me what to do with it, I'll tell you what happened. Is that fair? Fair enough? Terrific. This guy, The Shadow, he says, "Okay, tell me what you *think* you know." So I started in. I told him I thought the notion of using nuclear weapons to prevent the use of nuclear weapons —*(To* AUDREY*)*—which is the system we depend upon—*(To them both)*—simply doesn't work, not in the *long* run, too many places where the system just plain breaks down! Breakdown, in fact, I said, seems built in. What we've got, I said, is a fail-safe built-in breakdown machine. He said: "So how can I help you?" I said I want to know where I've gone wrong. He said: "You're not wrong. You've *got it!*" (AUDREY *stares at him, stunned. To* STONE, *with a gesture toward* AUDREY) I would think my expression probably looked a bit like that! *(To them both)* I said, "Wait, hold on, you're telling me the system doesn't work?" He said: "Why are you surprised? That's what you told me." I said: "But I didn't think I was right!" He said: "Well, you are." I said: "Well then, how come you and I are the only two who seem to know it?" You know what he said? Hold on to your seats, folks. He said actually *everybody* knew. It was common knowledge.

AUDREY: . . . Dear, that makes no sense.

TRENT *(Excitedly):* That's right! Of COURSE it makes no sense! But WHY does it make no sense?

AUDREY: Well . . . *(Pause)* Well, because if everyone knows . . . that what they're working on doesn't *work* . . .

TRENT: . . . Yes?

AUDREY: . . . Why would they keep working?

TRENT: EXACTLY!

AUDREY: I assume these are people who can find other jobs.

ALEX *(Offstage):* DAD, CAN I ASK YOU A QUESTION?

TRENT: No! And stay out of here. Go to your room. *(Back to* AUDREY *and* STONE) All right. So I asked what you asked: If they know it doesn't work, why do they keep working? . . . *"Because they don't believe what they know!"* (AUDREY *stares at him blankly)* Look, look, they know it doesn't work, okay? I mean, they've run the charts, the projections, intellectually they are fine, they understand, *but* they just can't BELIEVE it! Why? Because it SEEEEEEMS as if it should work. It's worked so far, right? So why not forever? You see? Logic! Worst thing that's ever *happened* to man! Oh, my God!

AUDREY: What?

TRENT: Down in Washington? Where I went to interview all these guys? There was something on their walls. I mean, each one had it. And I remember thinking: I wonder if these guys belong to some kind of club. Anyway, I didn't give it too much thought . . . Other guys, they put up posters of Bo Derek. These guys—they had Escher prints! *(Pause)* The Shadow! Let me show you how he got in touch with me! *(Looks up)* DOWN!

The photograph of the "crazy crate" descends on wires.

AUDREY *(To audience):* Aren't playwrights' houses *wonderful!*

TRENT: Look. You see? It doesn't work! And yet it *does.* It's not possible! And yet it *is.*

AUDREY: How does one *construct* an object like this?

TRENT: Not quite sure.

AUDREY: I'd love one in my office.

TRENT: So would I. Here's the Escher print they all had. DOWN!

Another hugely oversized print descends on wires, this one larger even than the first. AUDREY *stares up, puzzled.*

AUDREY: Dear, what's happened to your second floor? *(Now she sees the picture)* . . . Well, there's something very wrong with this.

They stare at the picture.

This is the picture that descends:

See Back Endpaper

AUDREY: I'm afraid I'm quite confused. How does one get the water to flow both up and down?

TRENT: It's a puzzler. *(Snaps his fingers, and the Escher print disappears)*

AUDREY: Thank you, dear.

TRENT: Okay, what he said so far, that the system doesn't work, that I can accept. But I said, "Surely, not *everyone* is like this. *Some* must believe what they know. You, for instance." "Absolutely," he said. "So, then, why are *you* working on it?" And he grinned . . . and said, *"Guess." (Silence)* Well, I was stumped. So I went back to the very first question I'd asked him, weeks before: "If the system doesn't work, why do we need more weapons?" His answer remained the same: we need more so we can strike first.

AUDREY: What!

TRENT: It's a defensive act.

AUDREY: Hitting someone first is a *defensive* act?

TRENT: If you know he's planning to hit you.

AUDREY: Why would he be planning to hit you?

TRENT: Because he thinks you're planning to hit him.

AUDREY: Well . . . he's *right.*

TRENT: There you are.

AUDREY: Dear, by this scheme, nobody does anything *offensive.*

TRENT: Exactly. Every act of aggression is defensive here. It's a completely moral system!

AUDREY: Well, something's wrong with it!

TRENT: I know.

AUDREY: Not quite sure what.

TRENT: It's a puzzler! *(To* STONE) So I said to him, "This is crazy, this is suicidal! If we strike first, they'll just retaliate, and wipe us out in return!"

AUDREY: THAT'S what's wrong with it!

TRENT: That's just one of them.

AUDREY: With one like that, you don't *need* any more.

TRENT: Exactly! And he agreed! *"That's why we've abandoned deterrence." (Looks to* AUDREY *for her response)*

AUDREY: . . . What?

TRENT: Exactly! WHAT? I mean, even if deterrence *doesn't* work, it works a *bit.* You don't just chuck it out, not without a substitute! Not a substitute, he said. An *improvement!* . . . And he grinned and said: "It seems, at least in theory, that a better mousetrap has been designed!" . . . Look, he said, an attack by us right now is suicidal because the enemy can always retaliate and wipe us out. However—what if we could *prevent* retaliation? "Well, in the future," he said, "which is what we're working toward, we think it may be possible, technologically, to do just this. And if we *can,* even if for the briefest time, a week, a month, create some kind of invulnerable window shade allowing our missiles out but nothing in, a kind of 'ion curtain'—incoming missiles hit it, bam! they disintegrate; then, in that brief moment of invulnerability, we can just . . . *take care of things.*"

AUDREY: That's barbaric!

TRENT: Ahhhh! Watch! No! Not at all! It's *defensive!* It's defensive because the Russians are working on the very same plan!

AUDREY: How do we know?

TRENT: Well, if *we* are, they *have* to be. Just in case *we* are. Which means *they* are—you see? Defensive! Again, a completely moral system. *(To STONE)* I *told* you this was fun! *(To AUDREY)* BUT! *(To STONE)* Here's the best part. *(To AUDREY)* Here's the *twist!* Even *this* doesn't work. *(To them both)* Watch! Let's say this ion curtain has been built and Sears has it, we call up and order one. Two weeks for delivery, they say. Well, that's not so bad, so we say send it on. PROBLEM: Surely the Soviets know somebody who works for Sears. "Psst! Guess what the Americans have just ordered!" Well! The Soviets know what's in store for them if we get this thing. Which means they have got to preempt. Which means we must PRE-preempt! We're right back where we started! You cannot beat the system, not from within; it simply doesn't work, *cannot* work, not in ANY permutation! It's that goddamn Escher print. "Right!" he said. And I could see his eyes—they were on FIRE! I mean, this man was *excited!* I thought, Am I dreaming this? This makes no sense! *(Pause)* And a moment later he was gone, in the fog, by the bandstand.

Long silence.

AUDREY: Dear, there's something very *wrong* here, something . . . you have *missed,* I think, I couldn't . . . say, of course, just *what,* I'm not an expert, dear, but clearly somewhere in your research you've gone wrong, that's just obvious, because this just makes no sense, as you yourself have even pointed out. *(Pause)* I mean, the world you are describing, dear, this is not a world I know. Furthermore, it's not a world I *care* to know, that's the truth, dear, I don't want to know any more. I think I need some air . . . Perhaps a stroll across the field! It's such a lovely day. Not the sort of day one wants to spend inside! *(She smiles and goes to get her purse. She stops near* STONE. *Pause)* Mr. Stone, if you would be so kind as to help him. Show him where he's wrong. I don't think I can be much more help to him on this . . . Not right now. I need to think this through. *(She stares at* TRENT. *Pause)* Keep with it, dear. *(She walks out. Long pause)*

TRENT: Is this what you mean by doom? That no one will believe?

STONE: Not quite. *(He smiles ever so faintly. Then he rises and pours himself a glass of iced tea)*

TRENT: Look, Stone, I am stumped, all right? I am at the end! What the hell was The Shadow up to? And why have you picked me for this?

STONE *stares at him. Pause.*

STONE: Have you ever been to the South Pacific?

TRENT *(Puzzled):* No.

STONE: Remarkable place! Beautiful beyond imagining! The imagination belittles its beauty. *(Pause)* Anyway, I was there in the early fifties. A close friend of mind was involved in our nuclear tests and asked if I'd like to go along on the viewing ship. It was not inappropriate for me to be there, for among my many financial interests at that time was a laboratory and development center. It was in Utah.

TRENT: . . . You make weapons?

STONE *(Slight smile):* I used to. *(Pause)* In any event, there we were on this ship, this battleship, not too far from where the detonation was to take place, which was near an island known, interestingly enough, as Christmas Island. *(Smiles. Pause)* We'd been told the bomb was to be a small one, and so none of us was particularly worried. Even though I'd never seen one go off, I figured, well, these people must know what they are doing! *(Pause)* Actually, the truth is I was in a kind of funk! That's because I hadn't come all this way just to see a *little* bomb! This one was ten kilotons, smaller even than the bomb at Hiroshima! These bombs were classified as *tactical* weapons. These are weapons you would use in combat. And, quite frankly, I was disappointed. I wanted some BIG-time stuff, and I'm not ashamed to say it, either. There's a glitter to nuclear weapons. I had sensed it in others and *felt it in myself.* If you come to these things as a scientist, it is irresistible, to feel it's there in your hands, so to speak, the ability to release this energy that fuels the stars! . . . to make it do your bidding! to make it perform these miracles! to lift a million tons of rock into the sky. And all from a thimbleful of stuff. *Irresistible! (Pause)* Well, we were standing by the railing when the countdown came on, we could hear it over the P-A. We'd all been adequately briefed, and we were in suits, some kind of lead, tinted visors on our helmets. And then I saw these . . . *birds.* Albatrosses! Phenomenal creatures, truly! They'd been flying beside the ship for days, accompanying us to the site, so to speak. Watching them was a wonder! *(Pause. Then in a tone of great amazement)* And suddenly I could see that they were smoking. Their feathers were on fire! And they were doing cartwheels . . . The light persisted for some time. It was instantaneously bright, and lingered, long enough for me to see the birds crash into the water. (ALEX *has come in unobserved by the others, and stands to the side, listening)* They were sizzling. Smoking! They were not vaporized, it's just that they were absorbing such intense radiation that they were being consumed by the heat! And so far there'd been no shock, none of the blast damage we talk about when we discuss the effects of these bombs. Instead, there were just these smoking, twist-

ing, fantastically contorted birds crashing into things . . .
And I could see vapor rising from the inner lagoon as the
surface of the water was heated by the intense flash. *(Pause)*
Well, I'd never seen anything like this in my life! . . . And I
thought: *This is what it will be like at the end of time. (Pause)*
And we all felt . . . the *thrill* of that idea. *(Long pause.*
STONE *stares at* TRENT, *who stares back at him in horror)* This
is your son, I believe. (TRENT *turns toward his son in horror.*
ALEX *looks frightened)* I've never met the lad, though of
course I heard you speak of him many years ago. I guess he
must be . . . eleven now. (TRENT *turns toward* STONE.
TRENT *seems stunned by this last remark. To* ALEX) I met your
father shortly after you were born.

TRENT *is reeling now. He stares from one to the other.*

ALEX: Was that a movie you saw?

STONE: Just now? Describing? (ALEX *nods)* Yes. A movie.
(ALEX *nods and leaves.* TRENT *stares out, stunned. The lights
start to fade on everything but* TRENT) I think I'm going to
have some more iced tea! *(He crosses to the pitcher and pours
himself a glass of tea. Soon* STONE *is but a shape in the dark)*

Light on TRENT.

TRENT: Now I know where we met! . . . It was at *our* place,
our apartment! We were living in the city then, and some
friends came by to see our child, he'd just been born; obviously, one of them brought Stone—who? doesn't matter, Stone
was there, I can see him, in a corner, *listening,* as I . . . tell.
(Pause) But *evil*? *(Long pause)* Our son had just been born.
We'd brought him home. He was what, five days old, I guess.
(Pause) And then one day my wife went out . . . And I was
left alone with him. And I was very excited. Because it was the
first time I was alone with him. And I picked him up, this tiny
thing, and started walking around the living room. We lived on
a high floor, overlooking the river, the Hudson. Light was

streaming in; it was a lovely, lilting autumn day, cool, beautiful. And I looked down at this tiny creature, this tiny thing, and I realized . . . *(Pause)* I realized I had never had anyone completely in my power before! . . . And I'd never known what that *meant!* Never felt anything remotely like that before! And I saw I was standing near a window. And it was open. It was but a few feet away. And I thought: I could . . . *drop him out!* And I went *toward* the window, because I couldn't believe this thought had come into my head—*where had it come from?* Not one part of me felt anything for this boy but love, not one part! My wife and I had planned, we were both in love, there was no anger, no resentment, nothing dark in me toward him at all, no one could ever have been more in love with his child than I, as much yes, but not more, not more, and I was thinking: I can throw him out of here! . . . and then he will be falling ten, twelve, fifteen, twenty stories down, and as he's falling, I will be *unable to get him back!* . . . And I felt a *thrill!* I FELT A THRILL! IT WAS THERE! . . . And, of course, I resisted this. It wasn't hard to do, resisting wasn't hard . . . BUT I DIDN'T STAY BY THE WINDOW! . . . AND I CLOSED IT! I resisted by moving away, back into the room . . . And I sat down with him. *(Pause)* Well, there's not a chance I would have done it, not a chance! *(Pause)* But I couldn't *take* a chance, it was very, very . . . seductive. *(Pause. He looks at* STONE. *The lights come back a bit.* STONE *is sipping his tea, eyes on* TRENT*)* If doom comes . . . it will come in *that* way.

STONE: I would think.

Pause.

TRENT: You want it to come, don't you!

STONE: What?

TRENT: Doom. You'd like to see it come!

STONE: No-no, of course not, that's ridiculous. *(He sips)* I just know that if it did, it would not be altogether without interest. I mean, it has its appeal, that's all I mean. It arouses my *curiosity.* *(Smiles)* But then, many things arouse my curiosity. Mustn't make too much of it. This is really good iced tea! My compliments to your wife. I think the secret is fresh mint, nothing like fresh mint; if you don't mind, I shall pick some from your garden when I leave. *(Pause)* I'm glad you've taken this job.

TRENT: Don't you understand, I can't write this play! Really, that's the truth, it is totally beyond me!

STONE *puts his hands on* TRENT's *shoulders.*

STONE *(Warmly):* Work on it.

He turns and starts out. At the rear of the room, by the window, he stops and looks out. Then he looks back at TRENT.

The lights go nearly to black on everything but TRENT *and the field outside the house. In this darkened room,* STONE *is but a shadowy presence. The curtains on the rear window flutter.* TRENT *stares out, lost in thought. Through the rear window,* ANN *can be seen strolling out across the bright field, hand in hand with* ALEX.

Curtain

Crazy Crate, photograph by Dr. Cochran